TALK IT THROUGH!

TALK IT THROUGH!

Listening, Speaking, and Pronunciation 2

Joann Rishel Kozyrev

University of California, Santa Barbara
International Programs

Marni Baker

University of Pennsylvania
English Language Program

Houghton Mifflin Company   Boston New York

Director of ESL Programs: **Susan Maguire**

Senior Associate Editor: **Kathy Sands Boehmer**

Editorial Assistant: **Manuel Muñoz**

Senior Project Editor: **Kathryn Dinovo**

Senior Cover Design Coordinator: **Deborah Azerrad Savona**

Manufacturing Manager: **Florence Cadran**

Marketing Manager: **Jay Hu**

Marketing Associate: **Claudia Martinez**

Cover design: **Ha Nguyen**

Cover image: **Alexander Papaleo**

Photo Credits: Chapter 1 Nancy A. Santullo/The Stock Market; Chapter 2 David Pollack/ The Stock Market; Chapter 3 Deborah Gilbert/The Image Bank; Chapter 4 Lisa Quinones/ Stockphoto.com; Chapter 5 Mug Shots/The Stock Market; Chapters 6 and 7 Digital imagery © 1999 PhotoDisc, Inc.; Chapter 8 LWA/The Stock Market

Printed in the U.S.A.

Library of Congress Catalog Card Number: 99-71979

ISBN: 0-395-96072-X

23456789-SB-04 03 02 01

TABLE OF CONTENTS

www.hmco.com/college

Talk It Through! is designed to be a complete text for the middle to high intermediate oral communication classroom, and provides a framework to help students build both the fluency and accuracy of their listening and speaking skills. It was designed to completely integrate listening, speaking, and pronunciation practice, while allowing the teacher flexibility to choose the elements of the course that the particular students in each class need the most.

The text is based on a model of the development of oral communication skills depicted here.

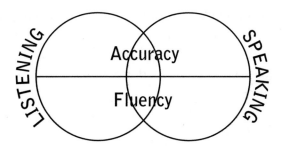

This model demonstrates how listening, speaking, accuracy, and fluency can work together to form the whole that is oral communication. The listening and speaking skills are represented by two overlapping circles. It shows that the skills are inherently related, although they sometimes operate separately. The line through the center of the diagram shows the division between accuracy and fluency. While these two elements interconnect, students experience the greatest improvement when they focus on one of these elements in a given activity in the text. This attention to focus provides students with attainable goals, allows them to build specific, useful strategies for improvement, and reduces the frustration that many students feel when faced with the overwhelming task of concentrating on meaning, vocabulary, fluency, and accuracy simultaneously.

Each chapter in *Talk It Through!* includes two complementary listenings on the same topic. The first listening is a scripted dialog, and the second features authentic unscripted interviews. The listening, pronunciation, and speaking activities that students complete are all directly based on these listening passages, and the models for the pronunciation and speaking skills practiced are gleaned directly from the listening passages. Listening skills emphasized in the text include listening for main ideas, details, emotions, and context. Next, students do pronunciation exercises drawn from the listening passages that they have just heard. The exercises include both listening and production practice. Within each pronunciation section, the production exercises lead from controlled information gap exercises to activities in which more student-generated speech is required.

Each listening is followed by a section entitled *Talk It Through!*, in which students develop speaking skills, including conversational, presentation, discussion, and interviewing skills. The chapters are sequenced so that earlier chapters support later activities. However, care has been taken to ensure that the chapters and activities can be taught in any order that the teacher chooses. An overview of the chapter sections follows.

Introduction

Introductory activities in each chapter are designed to introduce the topic that students will study in the chapter. They also help to contextualize some of the vocabulary and concepts used in the chapter. The teacher can select discussion questions or have students gather information from data in tables, charts, classified ads, diagrams, quotations, cartoons, and other sources.

Listening One

In each chapter, the first listening is a scripted dialog or conversation between one or more people. The dialogs are designed to be engaging and realistic while also providing language that students can later analyze when completing the related pronunciation and *Talk It Through!* sections of the text. For each listening, students complete global and closer listening activities designed to help them build their top-down listening skills.

Listening Two

The second listening in each chapter is an unscripted, authentic interview with people from all across the United States and Canada. The speakers offer a variety of regional accents and dialects. This second listening is more challenging than the first. Thus a teacher who wants to use just one listening from each chapter might choose the first listening for students who need more support and the second for students needing more-challenging material.

Pronunciation

Following every listening section is a Pronunciation section. In each chapter, one pronunciation section focuses on segmental pronunciation and one focuses on suprasegmental pronunciation. These sections begin with a reading that describes the pronunciation focus and then gives examples. Next, students complete predicting and listening exercises to build their bottom-up listening skills, as well as their self-monitoring abilities. Each Pronunciation section also includes a subsection that covers both controlled Practice Pronouncing as well as Communicative Pronunciation Practice. This will help students to begin to apply their developing production skills to their everyday speech, building both fluency and accuracy.

Talk It Through!

Each Pronunciation section is followed by the *Talk It Through!* section. This section focuses on building students' conversational and discussion skills. Each chapter contains two *Talk It Through!* sections, one focusing on a conversational skill and the other on a more formal speaking skill. For this reason, this text is the ideal conversation class text in the "Talk It" series. For each section, students can read a section that provides hints, strategies, and gambits that will help them to succeed at completing the speaking tasks at the end of the section. Often, students are referred back to a listening for an example of how to complete the task.

Further Practice

The Further Practice section ends each chapter and provides extension activities that teachers can use as follows:

- to recycle information learned earlier in the course
- to review the chapter's main points
- to provide Internet or out-of-class activities that students can do to look at a chapter's topic from a different angle

Further Practice activities do not have to be saved for the end of a chapter, but can often be used at any point in a unit.

At the end of each section is a Self-Evaluation checklist that students, as well as teachers, can use to provide each other with feedback about students' progress toward chapter goals.

ACKNOWLEDGMENTS

We want to express our gratitude to Susan Maguire, Director of ESL Programs at Houghton Mifflin, for her unwavering support and encouragement; to Kathy Sands-Boehmer from Houghton Mifflin and Angela Castro from English Language Trainers for their insight and editorial guidance; to Cindy Johnson, Publishing Services, for project management; and to Dana Knight Communications for audio production services. We also want to thank our colleagues and our students for offering their expertise, inspiration and valuable suggestions.

The following reviewers also contributed immeasurably to this text:

Edith Fusillo, Georgia Institute of Technology

Kathy Judd, Truman College

Patricia Pashby, University of San Francisco

Patricia Ramsey, William Rainey Harper College

Wally Sloat, William Rainey Harper College

Yvonne Sullivan, Cañada College

Ann Wennerstrom, University of Washington

Chart of Skill Coverage for Talk It Through!

	Listening Skills	Conversation Skills	Discussion/ Presentation Skills	Pronunciation
Chapter 1: People and Their Pets	Main Ideas Details	Making Suggestions	Organizing Information	Syllable Stress Thought Groups
Chapter 2: Hollywood	Making Predictions Listening for Context Details Note-Taking	Making Plans	Summarizing and Evaluating	Reduced Vowels Sentence Stress and Rhythm
Chapter 3: Identity: What Makes You Who You Are?	Identifying Context Main Ideas Detail	Asking Questions to Extend Conversation	Asking Questions in an Interview	Question and Statement Intonation –s, –es, and –ed Endings
Chapter 4: Environmental Ethics	Context Main Ideas Detail	Asking for Clarification	Using Words to Your Advantage	Reductions with /t/ Troublesome Consonants
Chapter 5: Private Lives, Public Information	Main Ideas Details Reasons	Expressing Anger and Frustration	Supporting Opinions with Reasons	Can and Can't Focal Stress
Chapter 6: Transportation Troubles	Main Ideas Details Making Inferences	Giving Directions	Persuasion	Consonant Clusters Linking
Chapter 7: Creating a Career	Emotions and Attitudes Details Main Ideas Guessing Meaning from Context	Describing Accomplishments	Tips for Answering Interview Questions	Using Intonation to Convey Attitude Vowel Length
Chapter 8: Science or Fiction?	Identifying Justifications Drawing Conclusions Main Ideas	Expressing Disagreement	Conducting a Survey	Vowel Sounds with Glides Intonation for Lists and Choices

One challenge in learning to pronounce English is mastering the many different ways that one sound can be spelled. One reason for the many different possible spellings is that the English alphabet contains only 26 letters, whereas most English dialects have approximately 39 sounds. To help you learn to pronounce sounds that are difficult for you, we sometimes use *phonetic spelling* in this text. Phonetic spelling is a system of spelling that provides one symbol for every sound in a language. *Talk It Through!* uses the Smith/Trager system for symbolizing the sounds of American English. The symbols used in *Talk It Through!* are shown in this box. Following the box is an exercise to help you learn to recognize these symbols and the sounds they represent.

Phonetic Spelling: Symbols for Sounds

Voiced Consonants		Voiceless Consonants		Vowels (Voiced)	
b	big	p	pen	iy	seen
m	man			ɪ	did
w	woman			ey	play
v	vowel	f	fight	ε	send
n	nice			æ	bad
d	done	t	top	ə	fun
z	zero	s	sing	ɑ	hot
l	light			uw	blue
r	red			ʊ	should
ð	that	θ	thing	ow	know
ʒ	usual	ʃ	shop	ɔ	brought
dʒ	job	tʃ	change	ay	fly
j	year			aw	brown
g	get	k	kind	oy	coin
ŋ	bring				
		h	help		

Voiced and Voiceless Sounds

Notice that in this chart, consonants are in two groups. The first is called *voiced consonants*, and the second is called *voiceless consonants*. Some sounds are made by vibrating the vocal cords; these are called *voiced sounds*. You can feel your vocal cords vibrate when you make these sounds if you put your hand on your throat while you speak. All vowels and the consonants in the left column are voiced sounds.

Voiceless sounds are made without any vibration of the vocal cords. If you put your hand on your throat while you say a voiceless sound, you will not feel any movement. The consonants in the middle column are all voiceless sounds. Notice that in the chart, sounds that are made in the same way except for a difference in voicing are placed next to each other.

Practicing Understanding Phonetic Spelling

Read the phonetic spelling for each of the following words, and on the line next to the phonetic spelling, write the correct English spelling for the word.

1. /dʒɑb/ _____

2. /tʃiypər/ _____

3. /sɛkʃən/ _____

4. /ədɑpt/ _____

5. /strey/ _____

6. /siyriyəs/ _____

7. /θɔt/ _____

8. /rəspɑnsəbɪlətiy/ _____

9. /pawnd/ _____

10. /əðər/ _____

CHAPTER 1
People and Their Pets

Chapter Highlights

▶ Listening to main ideas

▶ Listening to details

▶ Syllable stress

▶ Making suggestions

▶ Thought groups

▶ Organizing information

INTRODUCTION

Discussion Questions

Free write, tape record, or discuss your answers to these questions with others in your class.

1. Has anyone in your family ever had a pet? Why do you think people like to have pets?

2. Many people in North America have pets and treat these pets as members of the family. Are pets common in other countries you are familiar with? Why or why not? What kinds of relationships do people in these countries have with their pets?

Introductory Activity: Are Pets a Part of the Family?

Each year, the American Association of Animal Hospitals surveys about a thousand pet owners in the United States and Canada to find out how their pets are treated and whether they are considered "part of the family."

The questions in the following box are from the association's seventh annual survey. On your own, guess what percentage of pet owners answered yes to each question. Then compare your answers with the answers of others in your class and explain why you made the choices that you did.

Questions	% Who Answered Yes
1. Do you sometimes take your pet to work?	
2. Have you made sure your pet will be cared for after your death by putting it in your will?	
3. Do you take your pet on vacation?	
4. Do you feel guilty when your pet is at home alone?	
5. Do you give your pet toys to play with when it is alone?	
6. Do you include your pet when celebrating holidays?	
7. Do you pay extra attention to your pet when it is getting old?	
8. Did you make your pet a part of your marriage ceremony or take your pet on your honeymoon?	

Check your guesses against the actual survey results, and then discuss the following questions with others in your class.

Survey Results

Percentage of pet owners who answered yes to questions 1–8

1. 24%   4. 76%   7. 46%

2. 18%   5. 50%   8. 6%

3. 41%   6. 61%

Discussion Questions

1. Do any of these statistics surprise you? Which ones? Why?

2. How do you think that people in other countries would answer these questions? Would any of the statistics be similar?

LISTENING ONE ▶ Do You Really Want to Get a Dog?

Before You Listen: Brainstorming

Having a pet such as a dog or a cat has many advantages as well as disadvantages. With a group of your classmates, brainstorm a list of these advantages and disadvantages and put your ideas in the following chart.

Advantages of Pet Ownership	Disadvantages of Pet Ownership

Global Listening: Main Ideas

Listen to the conversation on the tape that occurred among three friends, Ashley, Courtney, and James. Ashley is thinking about getting a dog. Courtney and James both have very strong opinions about this idea. As you listen, decide whether their opinions are positive or negative, and circle the correct answer.

Courtney's opinion about Ashley's getting a dog: Positive   Negative

James' opinion about Ashley's getting a dog: Positive   Negative

Closer Listening: Details

Rewind the tape and listen to the conversation again. This time, pay special attention to the suggestions that James and Courtney make. On the following lines, list the suggestions that you hear. (You do not have to write down every word. Simply make a note of the most important words so that you can remember what you heard later.)

James' Suggestions	Courtney's Suggestions
_____	_____
_____	_____
_____	_____
_____	_____
_____	_____
_____	_____

Check your list with a partner. If you misunderstood or didn't catch any of the suggestions, listen to the dialog again.

Syllable Stress

A syllable is a part of a word in which all of the sounds are said without interruption. In English, each syllable must have one vowel sound and it may have one or several consonant sounds. In every word, one syllable is stressed more than any other syllables in the word—that is, it is longer, louder, and higher-pitched than the other syllables in the word. The words in the following lists are divided into syllables and the syllable that receives the most stress is underlined.

<u>time</u>	<u>sec</u>-tion	<u>o</u>-ver-board	o-<u>be</u>-di-ence
<u>pet</u>	<u>pup</u>-py	de-<u>ci</u>-sion	in-for-<u>ma</u>-tion-al

Stressed syllables are the basic building blocks of the rhythm and vowel sound system of English. If you learn to hear stressed syllables correctly, your listening ability will improve and you will be able to better understand people who speak quickly. You also must pronounce syllable stress accurately in order to correctly pronounce the rhythm and vowel sounds of English.

Practice Predicting Syllable Stress

The following ten words are from Listening One, which you just heard. Predict where each word is divided into syllables by drawing a line between the syllables. Then underline the syllable that you believe will receive the most stress. The first one is done for you.

1. <u>get</u>/ting
2. idea
3. almost
4. nights
5. responsibility

6. company
7. safer
8. people
9. second
10. thought

Practice Listening to Syllable Stress

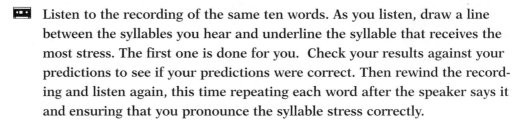 Listen to the recording of the same ten words. As you listen, draw a line between the syllables you hear and underline the syllable that receives the most stress. The first one is done for you. Check your results against your predictions to see if your predictions were correct. Then rewind the recording and listen again, this time repeating each word after the speaker says it and ensuring that you pronounce the syllable stress correctly.

1. <u>get</u>/ting
2. idea
3. almost
4. nights
5. responsibility
6. company
7. safer
8. people
9. second
10. thought

Communicative Pronunciation Practice

To learn new adjectives that are used to describe pets and practice syllable stress, follow these steps.

1. Look at this list of adjectives that can be used to describe pets. Add 5–10 more words to the list. You can find these new words by checking the pet section of the newspaper or searching for information about pets on the Internet.

   friendly, cuddly, magnificent, dedicated, intelligent, loyal

   _____

   _____

   _____

   _____

2. Learn the correct syllable stress for each word by asking an English speaker to pronounce the words for you or by consulting a dictionary pronunciation guide.

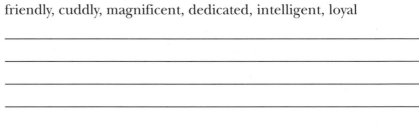

3. Look at pictures of people and their pets on the Internet or in magazines. Make up sentences that you think that these people might say about their pets using the words from the list. Share these sentences with others in your class, and as you do, be sure to pronounce the syllable stress in each of these words correctly.

Conversational Skills: Making Suggestions

Giving someone advice or making a suggestion is sometimes a little difficult. You want to help someone by giving good suggestions, but you must be careful that your suggestions are not misunderstood and that they don't offend the person whom you want to help. Here are some tips to remember when you want to make a suggestion to a person or a group.

- Use strong language only when you know the listener well, if you are sure that you won't hurt the listener's feelings, or if you feel that the listener is about to make a terrible mistake that could be very harmful.
- Listen carefully to your listener's responses to your suggestions. If your suggestions are not appreciated, consider backing down and saying, "Well, that's just my opinion."
- Use the following phrases for making suggestions.

	Strong	**Weak**
Positive	You should… .	If you think it's a good idea… .
	Go for it!	Maybe you should… .
	You're crazy if you don't… .	I guess it would be a good idea to… .
	Just do it!	If I were you, I would… .
	Don't give it a second thought!	It's your decision, but I think… .
	You have no choice. You have to… .	
Negative	Don't do it!	I'm not sure you should… .
	Have you lost it? You can't… .	I don't think I would… if I were you.
	You're crazy if you… .	Are you sure you want to…?
	You're not going to… .	It's your decision but I think… .
	You're not thinking of… .	
	You're not serious about… .	
	There's no way! You can't… .	

What can you do if someone is giving you advice and you want that person to stop? Usually, it's best to thank the person for the interest and advice by saying something such as the following:

> "Thanks for your suggestions. I need to think about this some more."

Or

> "Thanks for listening to my problem. I'll let you know what I decide to do."

Speaking Practice

In Listening One, Courtney and James suggest some problems that getting a dog might help solve, such as loneliness, difficulties in meeting new people, and personal safety. With a partner, examine the following situations and brainstorm a list of possible solutions to a similar problem. Then, role-play a conversation in which one partner explains the problem and the other suggests at least two possible solutions to this problem. Follow these steps.

1. With your partner, choose one of the following situations.
    a. A new student at your school has just arrived from his native country. At home, he has always lived with his parents, and they lived in a very safe neighborhood, where he never worried about walking at night or keeping his apartment secure. He tells you that he is a little nervous about living alone and admits that he doesn't know much about how to make sure that he will be safe in this new living situation.
    b. A student at your school is rather shy and has trouble meeting people who don't speak her native language. She really wants to find a way by which she can meet people who are good speakers of English so that her English will improve. She says that it has always been difficult for her to meet people, and now that she is worried about her English-speaking ability, it is even harder.
    c. A classmate seems worried and distracted lately. When asked if everything is OK, she says that some family problems are preventing her from doing well on her schoolwork. She admits that she hasn't been sleeping well. She doesn't tell you what the problems are but does say that she feels as if she doesn't have anyone to whom she can talk.

2. In the following chart, note at least two suggestions that you could give to the person regarding the problem situation selected from the previous list. Be sure to use useful phrases from the "Making Suggestions" chart.

First Suggestion for Dealing with the Problem	Second Suggestion for Dealing with the Problem

As you write your suggestions, discuss the following questions with your classmates:

   a.   In what situations do you think that it is appropriate to give strong suggestions?

   b.   In what situations do you feel that it would be more appropriate to use weaker suggestions?

3.   Plan and rehearse a role-play in which one classmate has the role of the person with the problem in the situation that you chose and other classmates make suggestions about how the problem could be solved. Don't write down every word that you plan to say. Speak from the notes that you made in the chart or imagine that the situation is real and then speak naturally.

4.   Perform your role-play for others in your class, or record it on audio tape or video tape.

5.   If you record the role-play, listen to it carefully to discover errors in making suggestions or in pronunciation. Perform the role-play again, correcting any errors.

LISTENING TWO ▶ A Part of the Family

Before You Listen: Discussing Statistics

Read the following statistics about the money that people spend on their dogs, and then discuss the questions that follow.

Dogs are considered by many to be "man's best friend." They are considered loyal, loving, and courageous members of the family. But at what cost? Every year, people in the United States spend more than five billion dollars on dog food and seven billion dollars on veterinary care for their canine pets. Added to this is the social cost of canine aggression. In one year, insurance companies in the United States paid 250 million dollars to victims of dog attacks. When other costs are included, experts estimate that aggressive dogs cost society one billion dollars a year.

Information from Stephen Budiansky, "The Truth about Dogs," *The Atlantic Monthly* (July 1999).

1. Why do you think North Americans are willing to pay such a high cost to keep dogs in their homes as pets?

2. This paragraph points out the negative costs of dogs to people and society. What are some of the positive effects that dogs have on people and society?

Global Listening: Main Ideas

As you listen, answer the following questions and discuss the answers with your classmates.

1. How does Dr. Glew feel about dogs? Why do you think so?

2. What is Dr. Glew's main point?

Closer Listening: Details

Dr. Glew believes that dogs play different roles for different groups of people. Listen to the tape again, and as you do, fill in the following table with a summary of Dr. Glew's description of the positive experiences that dogs give to older people and children.

Group of People	Positive Experiences
Older people	
Children	

Pronunciation

Thought Groups

When you learned to write English, you learned to write in sentences because a sentence is the basic unit of written language. However, if you listen closely when people speak English, you might notice that they don't always speak in complete sentences.

In fact, when we talk we use a different basic unit than the sentence. In this book, we call this basic unit a *thought group*. A thought group may be a sentence or a phrase, but it always has three things:

- A short pause before and after the thought group (sometimes very short!)
- Its own *intonation curve*, a pattern of pitch change that either rises or falls at the end of the thought group
- A logical idea

In the following sentence, taken from Listening Two, are six thought groups. The slashes indicate where the thought groups end.

> Well / if you're having a bad day and you're feeling sad / if you come home / the dog will have a tendency to come and sit with you and almost understand what you are feeling / put their head on your lap and sort of say "love me, because I love you" / and sort of make you feel a little bit better about life.

Thought groups are not as clearly defined as sentences are. A speaker who pauses more often when speaking could break the thought groups up as follows.

> Well / if you're having a bad day / and you're feeling sad / if you come home / the dog will have a tendency to come and sit with you / and almost understand what you are feeling / put their head on your lap / and sort of say "love me / because I love you" / and sort of make you feel a little bit better about life.

Learning to hear thought groups can improve your understanding of English because you can listen for the idea of each thought group. You can also hear the intonation and special stress patterns used in each thought group.

Learning to speak English by using thought groups can improve the comprehensibility of your speech a great deal! First, by putting pauses between thought groups, you make it easier for your listener to follow your thoughts. If you have trouble thinking and speaking quickly in English, make shorter thought groups. However, don't pause in mid-thought.

Practice Listening to Thought Groups

Listen to this excerpt from Listening Two. The thought groups in the first sentence are marked for you. Notice how Dr. Glew breaks her ideas into thought groups, and then mark each thought group with slashes. You might need to listen more than once.

> Well, / people / who have animals / often find that it provides a bond / that they may be lacking / with other human beings. Older people, the elderly, you know, the family has gone, everyone has left the house, and suddenly they're left alone, and the dog can fill the void of giving you something to do, something rewarding. You have to walk the animal every day, which is healthy for you, you have to brush the animal, which is good exercise, and you have someone to talk to, and they will look at you, and they will listen to you.

Once you have marked the thought groups that you hear, check your answers with a classmate. If you disagree on any answers, ask your teacher for assistance.

Practice Pronouncing Thought Groups

Rewind the tape and listen to the tape again, this time practice reading this paragraph along with Dr. Glew. Practice pronouncing the thought groups as she does. Then try reading the paragraph without the tape, using the thought groups that Dr. Glew does.

Communicative Pronunciation Practice

Follow these steps to see how well you use thought groups.

1. On audio tape, record a short one- to two-minute story about an experience that you have had with an animal that was your pet, that you saw in the wild, that you saw at the zoo, or in some other situation.

2. Listen to the tape and write down every word that you said (this is called *making a transcript*).

3. After you have written down every word, listen again and mark the thought groups that you used. Are there any places where your thought groups are too short or too long? Did you pause in places that might confuse a listener?

4. Use a different colored pen or pencil to mark your transcript with ideal thought groups.

5. Re-record your story, using the ideal thought groups that you marked.

6. Listen to both stories. Is the one with ideal thought groups easier to understand?

If you are having trouble with unnatural pausing and thought groups, you might want to talk with your teacher about strategies that you can use to improve in this area.

Presentation Skills: Organizing Information

Whether you are giving a formal presentation or expressing an opinion in a discussion, people will understand you better if you organize your ideas. Organizing your ideas by following these steps.

1. Tell your listeners your main point or idea.

2. Introduce a supporting point, and give all information related to this point before moving to the next supporting point.

3. Explain the next supporting point and all related information and ideas.

4. When you have made all of your points, you might want to restate your main point or idea.

If you are giving a planned speech or presentation, you can use notes or an outline to organize your ideas in this manner. Organizing ideas in unplanned speaking situations such as discussions or conversations takes more practice, but it is still very important. If you find it difficult to organize your ideas spontaneously, you can practice with a tape recorder. Speak on a topic for five minutes without planning what you will say. Then listen to see if your ideas are organized step-by-step.

Listening for Organization

Listen again to the conversation with Dr. Glew, and notice how her answers to the questions are organized so that she gives information about only one topic at a time. As you listen, make a note of each point that she discusses. The main point is identified for you as follows.

Her main point is that dogs have a special bond with human beings.

Her first example of this bond is how dogs help _____.

Her second example is how dogs help teach responsibility to _____.

Finally, she talks about how dogs _____.

Practicing Organizing Ideas: Impromptu Speeches

An impromptu speech is a short talk given with very little planning. Giving impromptu speeches is a good way to practice organizing information quickly. You can do impromptu speeches as a class or in groups. Follow these steps.

1. Each student in the class writes down three possible speaking topics on a piece of paper. Topics can be serious: "What is the most serious problem in the world today?" They can be personal: "Tell about your favorite animal and why you like it." Topics can even be silly: "Which is better—Coke or Pepsi?"

2. The students place all of the topics on a table, face down.

3. The first speaker takes three topics from the pile, chooses one, and then leaves the room to plan the speech. This person gets no more than five minutes to plan the speech.

4. Before the first speaker starts to talk, the second speaker takes three topics from the pile, chooses one, and leaves the room to plan.

5. The first speaker gives an impromptu speech of no more than five minutes.

6. The second speaker enters, and a third speaker chooses a topic. Repeat these steps until each member of the group has given a speech.

7. As a class, discuss the difficulties that each of you had organizing your ideas quickly. Also, share with your classmates any strategies that worked well for you.

Listening in the Real World

Television and radio news anchors are taught to use pauses between thought groups in order to present information in a way that is easy for their listeners to understand. Listen to a newscast and pay close attention to the pauses that the anchor makes when telling the story.

Now look in your favorite newspaper or magazine, and find a short article that is interesting to you and that you would like to share with your classmates. Imagine that you are a new anchor presenting the story on television. Mark the story to show where you will pause when reading it aloud. Practice reading the story aloud to make sure that the thought groups that you marked feel natural and that there are not too many or too few pauses. On audio tape, record the story that you prepared. Share your story with your teacher or classmates.

Self-Evaluation

Use the following checklist to evaluate your work in this chapter. Mark how well you think you have achieved this chapter's goals. Your teacher may also mark the checklist to evaluate your work. For areas marked as Needs Improvement, you should review the appropriate sections of the chapter to be sure that you get the additional practice that you need.

Goal	Excellent	Good	Needs Improvement
1. Listening to main ideas	___	___	___
2. Listening to details	___	___	___
3. Syllable stress	___	___	___
4. Making suggestions	___	___	___
5. Thought groups	___	___	___
6. Organizing information	___	___	___

Comments

CHAPTER 2
Hollywood

Chapter Highlights

▶ Making predictions

▶ Listening for context

▶ Reduced vowels

▶ Making plans

▶ Note-taking

▶ Sentence stress and rhythm

▶ Summarizing and evaluating

INTRODUCTION

Discussion Questions

Free-write, tape record, or discuss your answers to these questions with others in your class.

1. What genre of movies do you enjoy most? Independent movies or Hollywood blockbusters? Foreign movies or movies from your own country? Comedy, drama, action movies, or science fiction? Live action or animation? Why do you enjoy watching these movies?

2. What makes you want to see a movie? Do you ever see a movie because you read a good review, or do you like to see movies in which a favorite actor plays a role? Perhaps you are interested in seeing the newest special effects? What other reasons do you have for deciding to see a movie?

Introductory Activity: Reading a Schedule

Call the local movie phone directory or use the movie section from a local newspaper to complete the following activity.

1. Look through the movie section to choose three movies that you are interested in seeing.

2. Fill in the following chart with information about the movie that you want to see, the time and place that you could see it, the cost of the ticket, and the reason that it interests you.

3. After completing your chart, ask your classmates questions about the movies that they would like to see.

Title of Movie	Time and Location	Cost of Ticket	Why You Want to See This Movie

Before You Listen: Making Predictions

Read the following beginning part of a conversation between Allison and her classmate Steven. Fill in the blanks with what you predict will be Allison's part of the conversation. What do you predict this conversation is going to be about?

Steven: Hello?

Allison: _____

Steven: Yeah.

Allison: _____

Steven: Hey, what's up?

Allison: _____

Steven (sounds disappointed): I wish I could. I've already made plans. Hey, is it playing on Saturday? I could go to a matinee.

Global Listening: Listening for Context

Listen to the conversation between Allison and Steven and then answer the following questions.

1. What is the topic of the conversation?

2. What is the relationship between Allison and Steven?

3. What kind of movie is Steven in the mood for?

4. What kind of movie do they decide to see?

Closer Listening: Details

Listen to the conversation again. Write down Allison's responses. Compare what she says to your predictions. Then answer the following questions.

Steven: Hello?

Allison: _____

Steven: Yeah.

Allison: _____

Steven: Hey, what's up?

Allison: _____

Steven (sounds disappointed): I wish I could. I've already made plans. Hey, is it playing on Saturday? I could go to a matinee.

1. What class are Allison and Steven in together?
   a. art class
   b. cinema class
   c. They do not say.

2. When will the film festival be at Regal Cinema?
   a. Saturday only
   b. on the weekend
   c. all week

3. Why doesn't Steven want to see the first movie that Allison suggests?
   a. It isn't a comedy.
   b. The movie didn't get good reviews.
   c. He doesn't like reading subtitles.

4. What time does the movie begin?
   a. 7:00
   b. 7:30
   c. 8:00

After You Listen: Role-Play

Imagine that you will be calling a classmate to invite him or her to go to a movie. Make a list of three or more questions that you would need to ask each other. Then, using the chart that you completed in the beginning of the chapter, "call" one of your classmates and invite him or her to a movie.

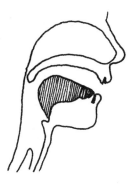

Pronunciation

Reduced Vowels

You probably already know that in English words, one syllable is stressed more than the others are. This means that this one syllable, when spoken, is longer and louder and has a higher pitch than the other syllables.

Stressed syllables usually have a full vowel sound such as /æ/, /ow/, /ɛ/ or one of the other vowel sounds in English. However, when a syllable is unstressed, it is pronounced too quickly and weakly for the vowel to be pronounced fully. Instead, native speakers of English will "reduce" the vowel sound so that the full vowel is not pronounced, and the vowel sound /ə/ (which sounds like "uh") is pronounced instead of a full vowel. [1]

The /ə/ sound is used for reduced vowels because it can be made in the middle of the mouth with the tongue in a relaxed position. Learning to understand reduced vowels can improve your listening comprehension. Pronouncing words with reduced vowels will help you to improve the fluency and comprehensibility of your spoken English.

[1] Not *all* unstressed vowels are reduced. For example, vowels in compound words and endings such as *-ly* and *-y* are often not reduced. However, many vowels are, including most unstressed prefixes and suffixes.

Practice Predicting Reduced Vowels

The following ten words are from the listening that you just heard. Look at the vowel sound in each syllable, and circle each vowel that you predict will be reduced to /ə/.

1. paper
2. festival
3. comedy
4. schedule
5. supposed
6. foreign
7. reviews
8. Saturday
9. drama
10. perfect

Practice Listening to and Pronouncing Reduced Vowels

Listen to the recording of the same ten words. As you listen, circle each vowel that is reduced. Check your predictions to see if they were correct. Then, rewind the recording and repeat after the speaker. Be sure to pronounce the reduced vowels correctly.

1. paper
2. festival
3. comedy
4. schedule
5. supposed
6. foreign
7. reviews
8. Saturday
9. drama
10. perfect

Communicative Pronunciation Practice: Catchy Titles

Directors, writers, producers, and movie critics all know that a good title can be very important to a movie's success. The title should get the audience's attention, fit the mood and story of the movie, and be easy to remember.

1. Practice pronouncing reduced vowels by recalling the names of movies that have multisyllabic titles, such as *Independence Day* and *Indecent Proposal*. With a group of classmates, make a list of these movie titles. Then read your titles to the class, pronouncing any reduced vowels correctly. Your class might want to count to see which group thought of (a) the most movie titles, (b) the most titles that no other group listed, and (c) the most titles containing reduced vowels.

TALK IT THROUGH!

2. Imagine that you are a script writer or movie director. In class or on audio tape, present a short description of the movie that you would like to make and the title that you would give the movie. Be sure to pronounce any reduced vowels correctly.

TALK **It Through!**

Conversational Skills: Making Plans

When people make plans to do something together, the conversation usually has three parts, as follows.

Part I: The invitation

One person suggests to another that they do something together.

Part II: Negotiation of the details

The people discuss plans, schedules, and other details.

Part III: Acceptance or refusal of the plan

The people decide that the plan will or will not work.

The three parts of the conversation are usually in this order, but the order is somewhat flexible. Here are some phrases that are often used when making plans.

Inviting

More formal:	Would you like to join me for… .
	We plan to… this weekend. We'd appreciate your company.
	Would you care to meet us for… ?
Less formal:	I was wondering if you want to… .
	Are you doing anything on Friday?
	I think I'll... You want to come with me?
	I'm planning on… .

Negotiating Details

More formal:	That time isn't very convenient for me. Is there another time that will work?
	That isn't my first choice. Are there any other options?
	That would be ideal.
Less formal:	I'm in the mood for… .
	I hate… . What else is there?
	I think that's doable.
	That will work.

Accepting/Confirming

More formal:	I'd be happy to join you.
	We plan to be there.
	It would be my pleasure.
Less formal:	Thanks for the invitation. That sounds great.
	Great!
	Sounds good.
	Count me in!

Refusing

More formal:	I'm afraid I have other plans, and I won't be able to attend.
	We won't be able to join you this time, but please keep us in mind next time.
Less formal:	I'm just way too busy right now. Sorry.
	I'm really tied-up this week.
	I can't do it this weekend.
	Can I get a rain-check?
	Maybe next time.

Practice Making Plans

Work with a partner, and choose one of the following situations. Imagine that you and your partner are making plans together, and role-play the conversation that might take place.

Situation #1

You and your partner would like to have dinner together. Talk to each other to determine (a) whether you want to order in or eat out, (b) what kind of food you want to eat, and (c) what day and time you will meet.

Situation #2

A person whom you work or study with calls you to invite you to attend his or her wedding. You don't know each other very well, but you would like to attend. You've never been to a wedding in this person's culture, so you ask some questions about the date of the wedding, what time the celebration starts and ends, what to wear, and so on. Then, you determine whether you will be able to attend and give your acceptance or refusal.

Situation #3

You and a classmate want to get together to study for a big test coming up in one of your classes. However, you are both very busy and it is difficult for you to find a good time and place to meet to study. Talk to each other, trying three or four different times and places before you find one that will work.

Cultural Notes: Making Excuses

In most parts of North America, people turn down an invitation by giving an excuse of some kind. People do this so that they will not appear ungrateful or offend the person who made the invitation. You will often hear the following excuses.

> I'm sorry, but I can't go. I have to drive my sister to the airport.

> Oh. Unfortunately, I've already promised my friend Sue I'd come for dinner.

Or at least:

> I'm sorry, but I'm busy tonight.

So how can you tell whether the person would like another invitation in the future? Usually, the person will let you know by saying something like the following.

> I'm busy on Friday, but I could come some other day. How about next weekend?

> I'd really like to visit, but tomorrow is out. Do you have time later in the week?

If you are unsure about whether the person would like another invitation, go ahead and ask! But if you get excuses the second and third times that you ask, you should probably extend your invitation to someone else.

Practice Making Polite Excuses

You have received the following message on your answering machine at home.

> "Hi! It's Chris. We met at the gym last week. I'm calling to see if you'd like to go to a movie this weekend. Call me back at 555-6879, and let me know."

On audio tape or an answering machine, leave Chris two different messages in which you explain that you can't go to the movies. In the first message, indicate that you would like to go some other time. In the second message, imply that you are not interested in going to the movies with Chris.

John Horn is a movie critic. He writes about the movie business for publications such as *Premier Magazine*, *Buzz Magazine*, and *The Los Angeles Times*. We spoke to Horn about what makes a movie a blockbuster, how a movie can make millions, and whether paying all those high salaries to stars is really worth it.

Before You Listen: Understanding Movie Industry Jargon

Read the following paragraph and discuss the meanings of the underlined words with your classmates. When you are certain of the meanings, discuss with your classmates a movie that you have seen recently, and try to use the underlined words in your conversation.

The <u>stars</u> were out last night to celebrate Brittany Taylor in the <u>leading</u> role of Hollywood Studio's <u>blockbuster</u> movie *Oceanic*. They were joined by the movie's <u>director</u>, writers, and <u>producer</u>, who seemed pleasantly surprised at the wide range of <u>demographics</u> that the movie appeals to and by the huge <u>box-office success</u> of their latest project. <u>Movie critics</u> are raving about the young actor, and <u>audiences</u> are seeing the movie in large numbers. <u>Ticket sales</u> for the <u>opening weekend</u> earned more than 20 million dollars.

Global Listening: Main Ideas

Before you listen to the interview with John Horn for the first time, read this list of possible questions that he might be asked. As you listen, check off each question that John Horn actually answers in the interview.

_____ 1. How much money does a producer or studio usually spend to make a blockbuster?

_____ 2. Why do movie stars get such high salaries?

_____ 3. What makes a movie a blockbuster?

_____ 4. What was the most popular movie ever?

_____ 5. What genres of movies are the most popular?

_____ 6. How much do special effects cost, and are they worth it?

Note-Taking

Practicing your note-taking skills can tell you a lot about your listening ability and can help you to improve it. You can use your notes to test how much of the information you hear that you are able to understand. You can also make notes of words that you are unsure of to check the correct spelling and meaning later. Here are some hints to help you take better notes.

- Do not try to write every word that you hear. Write only enough to remind you of what you heard.
- Use abbreviations whenever possible, but make sure that you will understand your abbreviations if you look at your notes several hours later.
- Use symbols such as arrows, underlining, circles, and so on to show relationships between ideas.
- Use question marks to remind yourself of parts of your notes that you are unsure of. You can check parts with question marks after you are finished taking notes.

Closer Listening: Practicing Note-Taking

Listen to the interview with John Horn a second time, and on your own paper, make notes of the main ideas and of as many details that you can while you listen. It might help you take notes if you use the main ideas from the questions that you identified in "Global Listening" to guide you.

After You Listen: Note-Taking Quiz

To check how complete your notes are, use your notes to answer the following questions.

Questions about the Main Ideas in the Interview

1. Why do some Hollywood actors make so much money?

2. To whom must a movie appeal if it is to become a blockbuster?

3. What is the one rule in Hollywood that everyone knows?

4. What genre of movies is the most popular and makes the most money?

Questions about the Details of the Interview

1. How many millions of dollars do some stars earn for appearing in one movie?

2. When is it most important that a movie attract an audience?

3. List three or more demographic groups that John Horn mentions.

4. Name two movies that people in Hollywood thought would be failures.

5. How much profit does the Disney Company usually make on a movie?

6. What movie made a billion dollars for the Disney Company?

Pronunciation

Sentence Stress and Rhythm

To understand how the rhythm of English should sound, imagine a drummer. The drummer can beat the drum with a very regular rhythm, making each beat equally loud and with the same amount of time between beats. This would sound like

DUM DUM DUM DUM DUM

However, usually the drummer makes some loud beats and some soft beats. Often the loud beats have the same amount of time between them, but between two loud beats there might be one, two, or more soft beats. And sometime there might be no soft beats between two loud beats. This might sound like

DUM DUM dida DUM didi DUM da DUM

When the drummer plays in this way, the rhythm is similar to the rhythm of spoken English.

Learning to correctly pronounce the rhythm of English is often one of the best ways to improve the comprehensibility of your speech. Two things cause the rhythm of North American English: stressed words and timing.

Stressed Words

Not every word in a sentence is stressed equally. Content words, which carry the most information, are heavily stressed on their stressed syllables. Function words, which give grammatical structure to a sentence, are usually unstressed. For example, in the following sentence the syllables in CAPITAL LETTERS are stressed:

> EVery COUple of YEARS a HOLlywood MOVie BREAKS ALL the RULES.

Content words include nouns, verbs, adjectives, and some pronouns (*this, that, these, those, yours, mine, ours, theirs, myself, yourself, himself, herself, itself, ourselves, yourselves, themselves*).

Timing

English is a stress-timed language, which means that there is equal time between each stressed syllable in a phrase or sentence. This means that it takes the same amount of time to say each "chunk" of this sentence:

> EVery |COUple of |YEARS a |HOLlywood |MOVie |BREAKS |ALL the |RULES.

So, it takes just as long to say the three syllables of "couple of" as it does to say the single syllable "breaks." To make this kind of timing possible, unstressed words and syllables must be pronounced very quickly.

How Important Is Sentence Rhythm?

Look at the following two excerpts from the interview with John Horn. In the first excerpt, function words have been deleted. In the second, content words have been deleted. Try to fill in the missing words in each excerpt.

Excerpt #1

_____ star _____ worth his _____ her salary _____ _____ fact _____ deliver _____ audience. There _____ _____ lot _____ examples _____ stars who cost _____ lot _____ money who _____ deliver _____ audience.

Excerpt #2

_____ it _____ is for a _____ to _____ to _____ the _____ would _____ a _____ _____ of _____. And _____

_____ really _____ is _____ _____ _____, _____, _____, _____ _____, even a _____ of _____ _____ will _____ _____ in and _____ the _____.

You probably found that it is easier to guess function words that have been deleted (in excerpt #1) than content words that have been deleted (in excerpt #2).

Practicing Listening to Sentence Rhythm

Follow the following steps to practice listening to sentence rhythm.

1. Now listen to these two excerpts on the audio tape. Try to fill in the correct missing words. You might need to pause the tape often, especially for excerpt #2, since content words are usually longer and take more time to write than function words.

2. When you have filled in all of the missing words, use a highlighter, colored pencil, or colored pen to mark the stressed syllables in these excerpts. Listen carefully to hear that generally the same amount of time lapses between each stressed syllable.

3. Listen to the recording again. This time, pay attention to the rhythm of the excerpts. Can you hear how the function words and unstressed syllables are said more quickly than the stressed syllables?

Practice Pronouncing Sentence Rhythm

Follow these steps to practice pronouncing sentence rhythm.

1. Make a short recording of two or three sentences of your own speech. Do _not_ write down what you will say before speaking. Just answer these questions on the tape recorder: "What is your favorite movie, and why did you like it?"

2. Write down each word that you said on the recording.

3. Mark with a highlighter or colored pen the syllables that should be stressed.

4. Practice using correct rhythm to say these sentences.

5. Record these two or three sentences again, using correct rhythm.

6. Compare your first recording and your second. Did your speech become more comprehensible?

Presentation Skills: Summarizing and Evaluating

When someone asks you about a movie that you have seen, a book that you have read, or TV show that you watched, what do you say? Most likely, you summarize the story or important points and give your own personal evaluation of whether the movie, book, or show is any good.

Summary

A summary is a short explanation of the most important points of something. It does not include the speaker's personal opinion.

Summaries are appropriate under the following circumstances:

- Telling someone the plot and main themes of a movie or book
- Relating the main points of a lecture or meeting to someone who wasn't there
- Passing information from one person to another
- It is important for you to show that you are unbiased

When summarizing, follow these steps.

- Use the third person, that is, use the pronouns *he, she, it,* and *they.*
- Choose verbs carefully to describe exactly what happened.
- Use connecting words such as *first, and then, next, after that, also* and others to help the audience understand your summary.

Evaluation

An evaluation shows your opinion about the value of something. To be believable and trustworthy, an evaluation should include both a statement of opinion about the thing being evaluated and the facts or other reasons that support the opinion.

Evaluations are appropriate under the following circumstances:

- Reviewing or suggesting a book, movie, or event to others
- Discussing the worth of doing or having a particular thing or event
- Giving your opinion about the usefulness or importance of something
- It is important for you to show that you are a well-informed, critical thinker who has thought carefully about something

When evaluating, follow these steps.

- It is OK to use the first person, such as *I think* or *It seemed to me.*
- Choose adjectives carefully to describe the qualities of the thing that you are evaluating.
- Use words such as *because, therefore,* and *for this reason* to support the evaluations that you make.

Identifying Summarizing and Evaluating Statements

Read each of the following statements. Write "S" next to statements that summarize, and write "E" next to statements that evaluate.

_____ 1. There were four main characters in the story.

_____ 2. Three of the actors were fantastic, but one was really not believable at all.

_____ 3. The star of this movie played a young man who lived with a roommate. His character was in love with his roommate's girlfriend.

_____ 4. The movie showed the pain that results when a person must choose between friendship and love.

_____ 5. The action in the movie was slow because the actors didn't play their roles very energetically.

Presenting a Review of a Book, Movie, TV Show, or Event

Practice summarizing and evaluating by presenting a short review to your classmates. Your review should include both a summary of the important parts of the book, movie, show, or event, as well as your evaluation of what was good and bad about it. Follow these steps.

1. Decide what you would like to review, and attend the event, read the book, or watch the movie/TV show that you chose. You might want to take notes, but if you do, be sure to keep notes that summarize separate from notes that evaluate.

2. Use your notes to organize your review. You might want to use the following outline.

   a. Introduce the thing that you will review. Tell your audience something interesting and exciting to get their attention.

   b. Summarize the story or the main elements of the thing that you are reviewing.

   c. Evaluate the thing that you are reviewing. What are the best parts, and why are they so good? What are the worst parts, and why are they so bad?

   d. Conclude your review with a final recommendation. Often, recommendations use *if* or *unless*. Example: "If you like romantic movies with happy endings, this is a great movie for you to see." "Don't watch this TV show unless you want to waste an hour listening to bad jokes and watching bad acting."

3. Do not write out the review word for word because it is too easy to lose your place in your notes while you are speaking. Instead, just write down a few words that can help you to remember what you planned to say.

4. Practice presenting your review. If you will be presenting in class, you might want to practice in front of a mirror.

5. Present your review to the class, or record it on audio tape or video tape.

FURTHER PRACTICE

Discussion

Hollywood is not the only place where movies are made. Many independent movies are made every year in other countries. To find out how much influence these movies have, follow these steps.

1. Visit a video rental store, and look at the new releases to find out which countries and minority viewpoints are represented.

2. With your classmates, discuss what you discovered and the possible causes behind these facts.

Self-Evaluation

Use the following checklist to evaluate your work in this chapter. Mark how well you think that you have achieved this chapter's goals. Your teacher might also mark the checklist to evaluate your work. For areas marked as Needs Improvement, you should review the appropriate sections of the chapter to be sure that you get the additional practice that you need.

Goal	Excellent	Good	Needs Improvement
1. Making predictions	_____	_____	_____
2. Listening for context	_____	_____	_____
3. Reduced vowels	_____	_____	_____
4. Making plans	_____	_____	_____
5. Note-taking	_____	_____	_____
6. Sentence stress and rhythm	_____	_____	_____
7. Summarizing and evaluating	_____	_____	_____

Comments

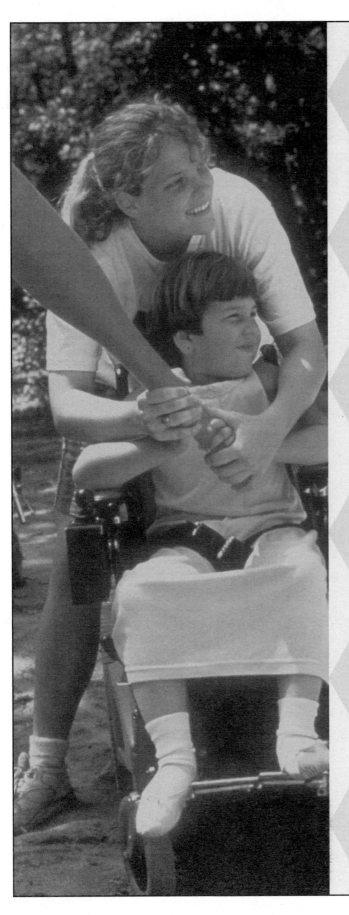

CHAPTER 3
Identity

What Makes You Who You Are?

Chapter Highlights

▶ Identifying context and situation

▶ Question and statement intonation

▶ Extending conversation

▶ Listening for main ideas and details

▶ –s, –es, and –ed endings

▶ Conducting an interview

INTRODUCTION

Discussion Questions

Free-write, tape record, or discuss your answers to these questions with others in your class.

1. How do you meet new people? Do you introduce yourself? Do you ask a friend to introduce you to people? What do you talk about when you meet people?

2. How do you feel when you meet new people? Why?

3. What are the elements of a person's identity? What does the word "identity" mean to you?

Introductory Activity: What Words Describe You?

If someone was describing you to others, what words do you think that person might use? What words would you suggest for the description? List in the following chart the words that you would use to describe yourself. Include nouns, verbs, and adjectives. If you aren't sure how to start, look at the example. You may use more words than the example does.

	Nouns	Verbs	Adjectives
Example	Sports Soccer Music	Play Dance	Vegetarian Thoughtful Active
You			

Exchange your list of words with a classmate. Use a piece of poster board or a large sheet of paper to make a poster using the words that describe your classmate. Your classmate will make a similar poster for you. You may add pictures from magazines or drawings to decorate the poster. The entire class should post the finished posters for all classmates around the classroom so that everyone can learn a little bit more about who their classmates are.

Before You Listen: Your Dream Identity

Young children are often asked, "What do you want to be when you grow up?" They answer, "a doctor," "an astronaut," "President." If you could be anyone whom you wanted, what kind of person would you be? What would you do? Would you differ a lot from the way you are now? Or would you be exactly the same? Take a few minutes to fill in the following chart with a description of your "dream identity."

Dream Identity

What Would You Do?	Where Would You Live?	What Would You Do in Your Free Time?

Next, discuss your dreams with your classmates. Then discuss the following questions.

1. What are the dreams of your classmates? How are they similar? How are they different?

2. What is each of you doing to reach your dreams, to make them reality?

3. What difficulties have you faced in trying to reach your dreams?

4. What experiences have you had that have helped you work toward your dreams?

Global Listening: Identifying Context and Situation

Listen to the conversation between Lauren and Josh, and answer the questions in the following chart.

Question	Answer	Why You Think So
Where do you imagine this conversation occurred?		
What do you think is the relationship between Lauren and Josh?		
Is Josh interested in what Lauren is saying?		
How is Lauren feeling?		

Closer Listening: Details

During the conversation, Josh uses a lot of questions to get Lauren to tell him more about the way that she is feeling. The following chart lists several of Josh's questions. Listen again carefully to the dialog, and write down Lauren's responses to Josh's questions.

Josh's Question	Lauren's Response
What's wrong? You look down in the dumps.	
What do you study?	
It sounds to me like you're in the wrong major.	
So why don't you change it?	
If you could be anything, what would it be?	
If you love it so much, why don't you go for it?	
Is that you or your father talking?	

Question and Statement Intonation

In this listening, you heard many questions and statements. In fact, questions and statements are a big part of almost any conversation. To be sure that your ideas are understood in a conversation, you must be able to use question and statement intonation properly. Intonation is the rising or falling pitch of your voice when you speak. Every thought group in English has an intonation pattern.

In English, intonation is commonly used to let the listener know when a question is being asked or when a statement is being made. Three basic patterns for questions and statements are available.

Statements

When making a statement, use an intonation pattern that falls at the end of the sentence.

I think it's a bad idea.

Yes/No Questions

When asking a yes/no question, use an intonation pattern that first drops and then rises. The change in intonation happens on the key word that the speaker is asking about.

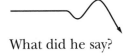

Do you think I can do it?

Wh Questions

In English, questions formed with the words *who, what, when, why,* and *how* have a special intonation pattern. In this pattern, the intonation first rises on the key word the speaker is asking about and then falls at the end of the sentence.

What did he say?

Intonation and Meaning

Using the correct intonation pattern for statements and questions *does* show your listener that you know the rules for intonation, but it expresses far more than that. If you use the *wrong* intonation pattern, you might give a listener an incorrect impression about your attitude or personality. Here are some of the misunderstandings that could occur.

Using question intonation with statement word order. This can

- make you sound unsure of yourself.
- cause a listener to think that you are asking a question. The listener might try to answer this "question." This can confuse you both!

Using statement intonation with question word order. This can

- make you sound rude or impatient.
- cause listeners to think that you're bored and don't want to talk to them.

Practice Listening to Question and Statement Intonation

Listen to the following sentences from the conversation between Josh and Lauren that you just heard. As you listen to each sentence, match the sentence with the correct intonation pattern in the list that follows. You will use each pattern more than once.

_____ 1. You look down in the dumps.
_____ 2. I'm looking at my class schedule, and it's terrible.
_____ 3. Too difficult?
_____ 4. What do you study?
_____ 5. It sounds to me like you're in the wrong major.
_____ 6. You can say that again.
_____ 7. So why don't you change it?
_____ 8. Wow, do you want to do that?
_____ 9. You'll think I'm nuts!
_____ 10. Is that you talking?

Intonation Curves

a.

b.

c.

Now, rewind the tape and listen to the sentences again. Repeat each after the speaker, being careful to match the intonation pattern that the speaker uses.

Practice Question and Statement Intonation

Mark in each of the following sentences the standard intonation pattern, and then practice reading each one.

Statements	**Questions**
a. He's got two brothers.	a. When did you arrive?
b. This is a new car.	b. Is someone going to help us?

1. What might a listener think if you say the statements with yes/no question intonation? Do people ever use this kind of pattern? Why?

2. What might a listener think if the questions are said with statement intonation? In what situations (if any) would it be appropriate to pronounce questions in this way?

Communicative Pronunciation Practice

To practice using question and statement intonation correctly, play a trivia game with your classmates.

1. Write three or more trivia questions, each on one side of a square of paper with the answer on the back. Or, select questions from a trivia game or book.

2. Sit in a circle, with each group member having 3–4 questions. One student asks the person to his or her left one of the questions on the question papers.

3. The person on the left of the questioner tries to answer the question. If that classmate does not know the answer, he or she should make up an answer to the question and then check to see if the answer was correct.

4. The rest of the class listens to hear whether the questioner and answerer have used the correct intonation patterns, asking the teacher for assistance when necessary.

5. Next, the answerer becomes a questioner and asks the person sitting on his or her left a question.

6. Repeat steps 4 through 6.

Conversation Skills: Extending Conversation

When you are talking to someone whom you don't know very well, it is important that you both ask each other questions. Otherwise, you might find that your conversation will end very quickly.

The first step is to learn to listen carefully to the new topics of conversation that a person brings up. Follow these tips.

- Remember that in English, new topics usually come at the end of a sentence.
- Sometimes an important noun phrase can give you a clue about a possible new topic of conversation.
- When answering questions, people will often give personal information that can be a source of new topics of conversation.

The next step is to ask questions. Imagine that a person you are talking to says the following during a conversation.

"Oh, I love this school. I've studied here for a year, and I think it's great. My classes are fantastic, and I joined the scuba club!"

In this statement, the person mentions

- her opinion about school,
- the length of time that she has been attending the school,
- her opinion about her classes, and
- her participation in scuba diving club.

For each of these topics, you probably can think of many informational questions to extend the conversation. For example:

- What made you decide to come to this school?
- Where were you before you came to school here?
- What classes are you taking?
- Wow, scuba diving! What's that like?

You might also want to relate the person's experience to your own:

- I'm so happy to hear that you like it here. I'm thinking about attending this school next year. Do you have any advice about applying?
- I came here last year, too! Did you live in the dorms last summer?
- I think that the classes are great, too. Did you ever have Dr. Kline?
- I love to dive. How can I join the club? Is it expensive?

The idea is to keep the conversation going so you can learn more about your new acquaintance and perhaps make a new friend!

With your classmates, analyze the following three statements for the topics or information that they present and write in the chart that follows the possible questions that you could ask to extend the conversation. When you have decided on several good questions for each statement, work with your classmates in pairs or small groups to role-play the conversation.

1. I didn't move to California until the early nineties. I grew up in northern Montana on my grandmother's ranch.

Topics	Possible Questions

2. I usually stay here on the weekends. I'm so busy during the week at school, so on the weekends I like to relax. I play tennis on Saturday mornings, and I spend the rest of the time watching videos, reading the newspaper at the coffee shop, and catching up on studying.

Topics	Possible Questions

3. I go to New York City about once a month. My uncle lives in Manhattan, so I stay at his place. I have a lot of friends up there from when I went to school.

Topics	Possible Questions

Before You Listen: Reading about Volunteering

To prepare to listen to this interview about volunteering, read the following short article twice. The first time, skim it for main ideas. The second time, discuss the questions that follow the article with your classmates.

Why Do People Volunteer?

A volunteer is a person who does something to help others without being paid for his or her time or expertise. Many volunteers will tell you, though, that they get something more valuable than money in exchange for the time that they spend volunteering. Susan J. Ellis of Energize, Inc., reports on many reasons that people volunteer. Here are just ten of those.

To feel needed
To build your resume
To share a skill
To make new friends
To get to know a community
To explore a career
To gain leadership skills
To feel good
To learn something new
To feel proud

Have you ever volunteered to do some service for others? Has a volunteer ever helped you? In the United States and Canada, many people would answer "yes!" to one or both of these questions. Volunteering comes in many different flavors. For example, people are often surprised to learn that in many small U.S. towns, all of the firefighters are volunteers, who are not paid for the service that they give their communities. And while many older people live in retirement homes, rather than with their children as in some countries, many volunteer their time to be with the elderly. These volunteers provide entertainment and companionship for the elderly. Other ways people volunteer include the following:

- Helping to make a community cleaner or safer
- Helping children with their school work or social skills

- Providing food, shelter, or care for the sick or poor
- Caring for sick or unwanted animals
- Teaching languages or other skills to people who need them but cannot pay for them
- Becoming involved in the government or the community
- Raising funds for nonprofit organizations
- Providing assistance to people affected by a natural disaster

As you can see, volunteering opportunities are available for people with many different talents. Many people believe that volunteering is good for the people who do the helping as well as those who are helped. Others believe that the government cannot solve community problems alone and that only people's willingness to volunteer their time and talents can make the world a more livable place.

Discussion Questions

1. Have you or anyone you know volunteered? If so, tell about this volunteering experience.

2. The article says that volunteering is common in Canada and the United States. In countries that you are familiar with, is volunteering common? What kind of volunteering do people in these countries do? Why?

3. Review the reasons for volunteering given in the previous article. Can you add any other examples?

4. Review the types of volunteering given in the previous article. Can you add any to the list? What volunteering opportunities are available in your community?

Global Listening: Main Ideas

📼 As you listen to Ali Feldman talk about her values, try to imagine what kind of person she is. Then work with a partner to write in the following chart the words that describe Ali.

	Nouns	Verbs	Adjectives
Ali			

Closer Listening: Details

📼 Listen again carefully as Ali describes her volunteering experience. Write down in the following chart Ali's answer to each of these questions. Then, for each of Ali's answers think of a question that you would ask her so as to help make the conversation more interesting and to find out more about her.

Question	Ali's Answer
How does it happen that you started volunteering?	

Your question for Ali about this topic:_____

Question	Ali's Answer
What are you doing in the way of volunteer work now?	

Your question for Ali about this topic:_____

Question	Ali's Answer
How do you find time for this, and how do you give up all that social life that goes along with being in college?	

Your question for Ali about this topic:_____

Question	Ali's Answer
What is it that volunteering gives you?	

Your question for Ali about this topic: _____

Pronunciation

–s, –es, and –ed Endings

Here are some simple rules that you can use to predict the correct pronunciation of

- regular past tense verbs (for example, We stopped.),
- present tense verbs in the third person (for example, She stops.), and
- plural nouns (for example, parties).

Before studying the rules, you might want to review the description of voiced and voiceless sounds in the To The Student section of this book.

Rule: If the base form of the verb or noun ends in a voiceless consonant, the ending is pronounced /s/ or /t/ because these are voiceless sounds.

stop + s	is pronounced	/staps/.
wish + ed	is pronounced	/wɪʃt/.
cat + s	is pronounced	/kæts/.

Rule: If the base form of the verb or noun ends in a voiced consonant, the ending is pronounced /z/ or /d/.

enter + s	is pronounced	/ɛntərz/.
rob + ed	is pronounced	/rabd/, spelled *robbed.*
game + s	is pronounced	/geymz/.

Rule: If the base of the verb ends in /t/ or /d/, then when making the past tense, pronounce the ending /əd/.

reflect + ed	is pronounced	/rəflɛktəd/.
extend + ed	is pronounced	/əkstɛndəd/.

Rule: If the base of the verb or noun ends in /s/, /z/, /ʃ/, /ʒ/, /tʃ/, or /dʒ/, pronounce the ending /əz/.

Business + es	is pronounced	/bɪznəsəz/.
Wish + es	is pronounced	/wɪʃəz/.
Change + es	is pronounced	/tʃeynðʒəz/.
Quiz + es	is pronounced	/kwɪzəz/.

Practice Listening to –s, –es, and –ed Endings

Read through the following four segments of the interview with Ali Feldman. Mark all of the –s and –ed word endings. Then, based on the rules in the preceding box, predict the pronunciation of the sound and write it above the word. When you have finished, check your predictions by listening to the tape again.

1. From a very young age, my parents always encouraged me to be involved with people who were less privileged than I was.

2. So, for example, when I went to summer camp one year, there were kids that were developmentally challenged, meaning they had different disabilities

3. like some kids couldn't walk properly, they were missing limbs, some kids had emotional problems, they had been abused,

4. and my parents had encouraged me to get to know these people because they thought it was important for me to learn that there are other people in this world who are not as fortunate as me, and what I can give to them I should.

Practice Pronouncing –s, –es, and –ed Endings

Read through the following conversation. Mark all the –s, –es, and –ed endings, and then discuss with a partner how each should be pronounced. Then, when you are sure about the correct pronunciation, read the dialog aloud or record it on audio tape for your teacher.

Jack: Hey, Amy, are you going to volunteer at the hospital this summer?

Amy: I can't. I worked there last summer, and the hours were too much for me.

Jack: You didn't like it?

Amy: No, I loved it. But I also have to work at my parents' restaurant, I'm taking two courses at the community college, and I need some time to relax.

Jack: Well, I'm busy, too, but I decided to do it. The director says that we only have to work five hours a week and she really needs help.

Amy: Who is the director now?

Jack: Nancy James. She visited my class last week and talked to everyone who was interested in the program.

Amy: Nancy James?

Jack: Yeah, she's new. She wants to make some changes in the way that the program is managed. You should talk to her. I know she's on campus Monday, Wednesday, and Friday at the Community Service Office.

Amy: The offices next to the Food Court?

Jack: Yeah, the building that used to be the physics lab.

Communicative Pronunciation Practice

When you think about people who have inspired and encouraged you throughout your life, do you think of any one of them as your role model? Prepare a short oral presentation for the class in the form of a timeline that describes the life of a person whom you consider to be your role model. During your presentation, you should use at least eight words that end in –s, –es, and/ or –ed. For example:

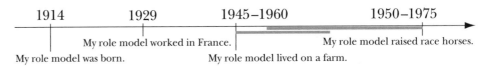

| 1914 | 1929 | 1945–1960 | 1950–1975 |

My role model worked in France.
My role model was born.
My role model lived on a farm.
My role model raised race horses.

TALK
It Through!

Interviewing Skills: Asking Questions in an Interview

When people hear the word "interview," they usually think of job interviews. However, we interview people in many other situations as well. For example, you interview salespeople when you are deciding what kind of car to buy, and you might interview a school official if you are trying to determine whether a school program is good for you to join. You might also interview a student or an employee at a school or company that you want to study at or work at. In most of these situations, you might say that you are "talking to" someone who is an expert or "asking a few questions," but in fact, you are conducting an interview!

Personal interviews are a great way to learn from someone who has first-hand experience with the information that you need. Whenever you interview someone, formally or informally, here are a few tips to follow. First, brainstorm a list of questions that you want to ask your interviewee. Remember, questions should encourage the interviewee to give you as much information as possible. Some useful types of question are the following.

Knowledge or Experience Questions

These questions ask your interviewee to recall information that he or she has learned or experienced. They include questions that begin with *what, where, who, when, why, how,* and *how much.*

Explanation or Comparison Questions

These questions ask your interviewee to give examples of or compare or contrast the information in their answer. They include questions such as these.

Can you give an example of ...?
Can you explain what you mean by ...?
Can you contrast that with ...?
Can you compare that to ...?

Creative Questions

These questions ask the interviewee to use creative thinking, logic, and problem-solving skills in her or his answer. They include questions such as these.

What would you do if ...?
What would happen if ...?
How do you imagine this would affect ...?

Opinion Questions

These questions ask the interviewee to give an opinion about or to critique something. They include questions such as these.

What do you believe about ...?
What is your opinion about ...?
Which is most important ...?

When you are creating your list of questions, you should *not* use the following question types.

Yes/No Questions

This type of question produces no discussion. An example of a yes/no question is the following:

Do you volunteer at the hospital after school?

Multiple Questions in One Sentence

This type of question confuses the interviewee because he or she won't know which question to answer. An example of a multiple question is the following:

Do you think that volunteering is an effective way to help people, and if so, why, and is there any kind of volunteer organization that you can recommend over the others?

Unclear Questions

This type of question also confuses the interviewee because he or she does not understand what you are asking. An example of an unclear question is the following:

> How about that after-school reading program?

Leading Questions

A leading question is not good because it gives the interviewee the answer rather than letting that person give his or her own answer. An example of a leading question is the following:

> Don't you think that volunteering is the best way to help the needy?

Once you have created a list of possible questions, follow these steps.

1. Assign each question a priority. Which are the most important?

2. Think about how long your interview will be. If someone you don't know very well is doing the interview as a favor, you shouldn't take too much time. However, if the person is trying to sell you something, such as a computer or a car, he or she might be willing to take more time.

3. Choose the questions that you will ask. Remember that you might have to ask one question to lead up to another question. For example, if you are asking someone about an organization that the interviewee volunteers for, you probably wouldn't start by asking, "Do you think I should volunteer here?" It would be better to start by asking, "What kind of volunteer work does your organization do?"

Identifying Good Interview Questions

Read the following two question lists, which were prepared for a 20-minute interview with a Tae Kwon Do instructor. Compare the good and bad points of each list of questions. Refer to the list of tips for interviews in the previous box if you need help.

List #1

Question #1:	Do you like teaching Tae Kwon Do?
Question #2:	What is Tae Kwon Do?
Question #3:	How did you get your start as a Tae Kwon Do instructor?
Question #4:	How about Karate?
Question #5:	What if I want to be a Tae Kwon Do instructor. What would I have to do?

List #2:

Question #1: Is Tae Kwon Do fun and would you recommend it to people who have problems with their backs, is it safe?

Question #2: Don't you think Tae Kwon Do is the most effective martial art for keeping in good physical shape?

Question #3: Can anybody learn to do Tae Kwon Do, or do you need special talent?

Question #4: Is Tae Kwon Do good exercise?

Conducting an Interview

Interview someone about something that he or she loves to do. You might interview someone who volunteers or teaches a class or who is a specialist in a certain field of study. You can interview someone who works at your school or lives in your community. You might even interview someone in your class. Try to find out more about what they do, how they started doing it, and why they continue to do it. Follow these steps.

1. Arrange the interview ahead of time. If you are having trouble selecting someone to interview, try asking your teacher or people whom you know. You can also check the local newspaper for information about people with special interests and talents. If you have Internet access, you might even interview someone on the Internet or through e-mail.

2. Plan the questions that you will ask. Remember the tips in the box on pages 46–48. If your interviewee wishes, you should give these questions to him or her ahead of time.

3. Take notes during the interview, but do not try to write down every word that your interviewee says.

4. Remember at the end of the interview to thank the person whom you interviewed.

5. In class or on audio tape, organize and give a short presentation summarizing the information that you learned in your interview.

Finding Similarities

When we form friendships, most of us look for people who are similar to us in socioeconomic status, education, lifestyle, profession, race, gender, and/or ethnicity. That is, we gravitate toward people who seem like us and away from people who seem different from us. In reality, however, many of the people who *seem* like us are very different in many important ways, such as the way in which they communicate, their life goals and objectives, and their personal interests and values. At the same time, many of the people who *seem* different are actually not that different at all.

Find differences in someone whom you think is very similar to you, and find similarities in someone whom you think is very different from you. Think about someone in your class or someone you know outside of class who seems to be very similar to you in lifestyle, profession, age, gender, race, and/or ethnicity. Complete the following chart, indicating how the person is similar to you and how different from you.

Similarities	Differences

Now think of a person in or out of your class who is very different from you in lifestyle, profession, age, gender, race, or ethnicity. Complete the following chart, indicating how the person is similar to you and how he or she is different from you.

Similarities	Differences

Discuss what you have written with a partner or a small group. Do you agree that most people choose their friends based on similarities such as gender, ethnicity, income, and/or education? Do you think that choosing friends based on these similarities is a good idea? Why or why not? As you discuss your ideas, be aware of your intonation for questions and answers.

Cyber-Identities

Read the paragraph in the following box, and discuss the questions that follow it.

Identity and the Internet

The Internet has become a popular way of communicating, and many people are revealing their identities on the Internet. Some of the ways in which people do this are by creating unique "screen names" that differ from their real names, joining newsgroups or e-mail lists on subjects of interest to them, and creating home pages that show and tell about the person's interests, concerns, activities, and other elements of their identities. Some people have very elaborate identities on-line that differ very much from their real-life identities. For example, a shy person might become very outgoing when sending e-mail to people whom he or she has met only through the computer.

Some people with disabilities, such as those who must use a wheelchair or who are deaf, really appreciate the Internet because it allows them to meet and communicate with people more easily and to share their thoughts and ideas without having the people that they meet always focusing on the disability.

Most people who use the Internet reveal the same identity on-line that they have off-line. However, some people tell others things about themselves that are completely untrue. They do this because the computer allows them to be anonymous— no one can check to see if the identity shown on-line is a true identity.

Discussion Questions

Find out how many people in your class (a) use e-mail regularly, (b) have home pages, and (c) have friends on the Internet whom they have never met in person. In small groups, talk about why people use the Internet for communication in these ways.

1. Why do you think someone would take on a "new" or even a "false" identity on the Internet? What are the advantages and disadvantages of Internet anonymity for communicating with other people under the following circumstances?

   a. For people who are learning English
   b. For people with disabilities
   c. For people who are shy
   d. For business professionals

2. How can you be sure that a person's on-line identity is his or her true identity? What should people do before meeting in person someone whom they have interacted with only on the Internet?

3. What is the attraction of meeting and communicating with other people on the Internet through e-mail and home pages?

Going On-Line

Spend some time looking at home pages on the Internet. Try to find home pages that show interesting aspects of their creators' identities. If your teachers or classmates have created home pages, you might want to look at their pages. Find one page that is particularly interesting to you and if possible show it or a printout of it to the class. Explain what you can learn about this person's identity from the home page.

Self-Evaluation

Use the following checklist to evaluate your work in this chapter. Mark how well you think that you have achieved this chapter's goals. Your teacher might also mark the checklist to evaluate your work. For areas marked as Needs Improvement, you should review the appropriate sections of the chapter to be sure that you get the additional practice that you need.

Goal	Excellent	Good	Needs Improvement
1. Identifying context and situation	____	____	____
2. Question and statement intonation	____	____	____
3. Extending conversation	____	____	____
4. Listening for main ideas and details	____	____	____
5. *–s*, *–es*, and *–ed* endings	____	____	____
6. Conducting an interview	____	____	____

Comments

CHAPTER 4
Environmental Ethics

Chapter Highlights

▶ Listening for context and main ideas

▶ Listening for details

▶ Reductions with /t/

▶ Asking for clarification

▶ Troublesome consonants: /r/, /l/, /θ/, and /ð/

▶ Using words to your advantage

Discussion Questions

Free-write, tape record, or discuss your answers to these questions with others in your class.

1. Who should be responsible for monitoring a company's environmental ethics? The company? Its employees? Its customers? The government? Why?

2. Should the environment be saved at all costs? In other words, should we be willing to slow down or stop human economic and industrial progress to protect the environment? Why or why not?

Introductory Activity: Discussing a Quotation

Read the following quotation from Chief Seattle, a famous Native American, and discuss the questions that follow with your classmates.

"Teach your children what we have taught our children—that the earth is our mother. Whatever befalls the earth, befalls the sons of the earth. If men spit upon the ground, they spit upon themselves.

This we know. The earth does not belong to man; man belongs to the earth. This we know. All things are connected like the blood which unites one family. All things are connected.

Whatever befalls the earth befalls the sons of the earth. Man did not weave the web of life; he is merely a strand in it. Whatever he does to the web, he does to himself."

Chief Seattle as quoted in *The Earth Speaks*. Steve Van Matre and Bill Weiler (Eds.) (1983). Warrenville, IL: The Institute for Earth Education.

1. What does Chief Seattle want us to understand about the relationship between people and Earth?

2. Do you agree with Chief Seattle's idea? Why or why not?

3. Do you think that people in North America are more or less aware of their connection to the Earth than are people from other cultures? Why do you think so?

LISTENING ONE ▶ Paradise Lost or Found?

Before You Listen: The Effects of Tourism

Think about your home country or city. What are its three most popular tourist destinations? Why do people visit those places? What are the positive and/or negative effects of this tourism on the local environment, culture, and economy? Complete the following chart with descriptions of your country or city's tourism industry.

Tourist Destination	Reasons for Visiting	Positive Effects of Tourism	Negative Effects of Tourism

Give a one- to three-minute presentation about the information in this chart to a small group of your classmates. When all members of your group have finished with their presentations, all members should compare charts and then answer the following questions.

1. What seem to be the common positive effects of the tourism industry?

2. What seem to be the common negative effects?

Global Listening: Context and Main Ideas

Listen to the following conversation between Terry and Jason, and then answer the questions that follow.

1. Where is this conversation taking place, and what do you imagine that this place looks like?

2. How does Terry feel about the new hotel and golf course?

3. How does Jason feel about the new hotel and golf course?

Closer Listening: Details

During the conversation, Terry talks about the possible positive effects of building the new resort and Jason talks about the possible negative effects. Listen to the conversation again, and write down these positive and negative effects in the following chart.

Positive Effects	Negative Effects

After You Listen: Discussion Question

Discuss the following question with your classmates. Use information from the listening to support your answer.

1. Whose argument is stronger, Terry's or Jason's? Why do you think so?

Pronunciation

Reductions with /t/

/t/ by itself is not a difficult sound to make. Many languages have this sound, and few students complain of trouble understanding or pronouncing it. It even is usually spelled like it sounds. However, in most North American dialects, the sound /t/ can be changed when it occurs near other sounds in a word or a phrase. Here are some of the common changes.

/n/ + /t/

When the sound /t/ follows the sound /n/ in a word, the /t/ is often not pronounced. For example:

mental	becomes	/mɛn-əl/.
didn't	becomes	/did-ən/.

VOWEL + /t/ + vowel

When the /t/ sound falls between a stressed vowel and an unstressed vowel, it is pronounced in a special way, called a *flap*. To many people, the flapped /t/ sounds like a /d/. Spanish speakers might notice that it sounds a bit like the single /r/ sound in Spanish. For example:

letter	becomes	/lɛd-ər/.
ditto	becomes	/dɪd-o/.
after	becomes	/æf-dər/.

BUT hotel remains /how-tɛl/ because in this word, the syllable after the /t/ is stressed, rather than the syllable before the /t/.

/t/ + /y/

When the /t/ sound is followed by the /y/ sound, the two combine to make the /tʃ/ sound. For example:

future	is pronounced	/fyuw-tʃər/.
got you	is usually pronounced	/ga-tʃə/.

Remember, this happens when /t/ is followed by the *sound* /y/, not necessarily the *letter y*.

You will probably be understood by most English speakers even if you do not pronounce the sound /t/ in these ways. However, you must learn to understand these pronunciations, as they are very common in North American English.

Practice Listening to Reductions

In the following excerpt from the conversation that you just heard, circle the /t/ sounds which you think that a North American speaker would reduce. Then, listen to the excerpt to check your answers.

> The Mayor wrote a letter that was published, I don't know, Saturday or Sunday. And, he said the new hotel and golf course would create 430 new jobs. And of course with all the tourists, businesses like restaurants and retail shops will do better as well. People are excited about it.

Practice Pronouncing Reductions with /t/

In the following dialog, predict where reductions with /t/ will occur in North American English. Mark these words. Compare your guesses with a partner, and then check your understanding with your teacher. When you are sure about where the reductions occur, perform the text with your partner on audio tape or for the class.

Susan: Hey Matt! What are you doing later?

Matt: I told Ann I'd meet her for dinner. Didn't you say you know Ann?

Susan: Yeah, we had class together last year. Where are you eating?

Matt: At Andy's. Do you want to come?

Susan: I'd like to, but I'd better not. I have to study. I've got to think about the future!

Matt: Not even just for dinner?

Susan: No. But if I change my mind, I've got your number.

Matt: Okay. Talk to you later!

Communicative Pronunciation Practice

Follow these steps to practice reductions with /t/.

1. Imagine that you are interviewing residents of Green Mountain, a small city in North America. You want to know how they feel about tourism in their city and the effects of tourism on the natural environment. Look at the following interview questions, and mark where reductions with /t/ would occur in North American English.

    a. What is your name?

    b. How old are you?

    c. What is your profession?

    d. Do you think that tourism is destructive to the local environment?

    e. What are some possible solutions to this problem?

    f. What is your opinion about eco-tourism?

2. Look at three people's answers to these questions in the following chart. Mark any /t/ sounds that you expect would be reduced in North American English.

Betty Jones	Peter White	Tom Little
• 40 years old	• 32 years old	• 18 years old
• Well educated	• A restaurant owner and a writer for the local newspaper.	• One of the city's brightest high school students. Works as a waiter in the summer at a local hotel.
• Professor at a local university. Set up the first environmental education center in the city.	• Excited about the new opportunities that tourism brings to the city. Not at all worried about the possible negative effects of the tourism industry on the environment.	• Upset at the destruction of the local environment but understands that a lot of people depend on tourism for their jobs.
• Very angry about the tourism industry's rate of growth and the negative effects of this industry on her city's future.	• Believes that increasing tourism will improve everyone's quality of life. Thinks that a lot of environmentalists are a little bit crazy.	• Thinks people in the city should get over their differences and work together to find a solution.
• Wants to stop tourism activity completely because it is destroying the city's natural beauty.		

3. Work with a partner or in a small group to role-play the interview. One person acts as the interviewer. The others play the parts of Betty, Peter, or Tom and answer the interviewer's questions based on the information in the previous chart. If you need to review interviewing skills, refer to the box in Chapter 3, page 46. As you ask and answer the questions, practicing the use of the /t/ sound and the flap or /d/ sound correctly. Record your role-play on audio tape, or perform it for the class.

Conversational Skills: Asking for Clarification

When having a conversation, you might not hear or understand what someone has said. This happens to everyone, even native speakers. In this case, it is appropriate to ask for clarification, that is, to ask the person to whom you are talking to slow down or repeat what he or she has said. You can ask for clarification by asking the person to do any of the following.

Repeat what he or she has said. For example:

I'm sorry, could you repeat that, please?

Excuse me, one more time, please.

Could you run that by me again, please?

Rephrase what he or she has said. For example:

I'm not sure I understand. Could you explain it another way?

I'm not getting it. (I don't get it). Could we go over it again?

Give more precise information. For example:

I'm not sure I get it. Could you give me more details?

I don't think I understand. Could you tell me a little more about it?

Tell you if your understanding is correct. For example:

You said … right?

You mean … correct?

Here are some typical responses for this type of request for clarification.

Positive: Exactly!
Right.
Correct.
Um-hmm.
Yes.
Yeah.

Negative: Well, not exactly.
Not quite.
No.
Actually, I meant … .

If you have misunderstood, people will often respond to your request for clarification by repeating what they have said.

Practice Asking for Clarification

Perform the following role-play with a partner. Character A calls Character B on the telephone to ask questions about a recycling program. As you have the conversation, try to use as many clarification questions and responses as you can.

Character A: A New Tenant in a Large Apartment Building in Center City

You have recently moved into a new apartment building, and you are confused about its recycling program. You have been saving your glass, cans, plastics, and newspapers in your closets, and you want to get rid of them. You have seen red and green plastic baskets in the hallway. You believe that these are recycling bins, but you do not have one, and you are not sure which days are pick-up days.

Character B: Director of the Center City Recycling Program

Your program offers recycling for glass and plastics. Glass is picked up on Tuesdays and plastics on Fridays. Glass is to be cleaned and stored in a red plastic basket. Plastics are to be stored in a green plastic basket. The baskets are free and can be picked up in the neighborhood at 3201 Lytle Street. Your program does not recycle newspapers. Newspaper recycling services are available at 3308 White Street.

Before You Listen: Interpreting a Cartoon

Look at this cartoon and answer the questions that follow.

© Wicks/Rothco. Reprinted with permission.

1. What is the problem represented by this cartoon?

2. What message do you think that the cartoonist was trying to express with this cartoon?

Cultural Notes

Read the information in the following box on the "throw-away society," and answer the questions that follow.

The Throw-Away Society

The United States has been characterized as a "throw-away society." At a rate that is at least twice as high as any other industrial nation, U.S. citizens purchase an enormous amount of goods and then throw them away. Every day, people in the United States produce over 430,000 tons of garbage. That's about four pounds of garbage per person per day!

1. What is meant by the phrase "throw-away society"?

2. Why do you think that the United States has become a throw-away society?

3. Have you seen evidence of the throw-away mentality in your own culture or in other cultures? Explain.

Global Listening: Main Ideas

Suzanne Stephens is a public relations representative at a waste management company. Her company manages both a recycling plant and a landfill to dispose of the waste created by the people and businesses in the community. She's concerned about the many ways that industry affects the environment—especially the issues that have come up as a result of economic growth in her region.

1. What are the two most important environmental problems that Ms. Stephens thinks people and businesses face today?

2. Will businesses willingly help to solve these environmental problems? Why or why not?

Closer Listening: Details

During the interview, Ms. Stephens gives her opinion on several topics. Listen to the interview again, and write down her opinion about the topics in the following chart.

Topic	Opinion
The growth of the waste problem in North Carolina	
Recycling	
Environmental laws enforced by the government	

Pronunciation

Troublesome Consonants: /r/, /l/, /θ/, and /ð/

Many students have difficulty pronouncing one or more of these consonants: /r/, /l/, /θ/, and /ð/. If you do not have these sounds in your native language, they might be very difficult for you to pronounce. However, if you learn how to place your tongue correctly and you practice daily, you can learn to pronounce them. If you have trouble with more than one of them, practice them one at a time, rather than trying to perfect all four at once. You should choose just one sound to focus on in these activities.

/r/

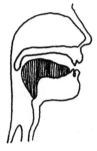

The /r/ sound is made by keeping your tongue in the middle of your mouth. The sides of your tongue may touch your back teeth, but the tip of you tongue should not touch anything. To help to produce this sound, try making the right and left sides of your lips rather tight.

/l/

To make the /l/ sound, you must place the tip of your tongue on the bump behind your top front teeth. The middle of your tongue should be pushed down into the bottom of your mouth. If your /l/ sounds too much like an /r/, try pushing your tongue further forward. It may even touch your upper teeth.

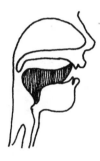

/θ/ and /ð/

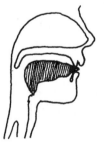

These two "th" sounds are shown together because they are formed with the same tongue placement; however, /θ/ is voiceless and /ð/ is voiced. You make these two sounds by blocking the space between your teeth with your tongue and then pushing air past your tongue and between your teeth. You should be able to see the tip of your tongue if you look closely in a mirror. You do not need to stick your tongue far out of your mouth, but exaggerating the tongue placement and pushing it far out between your teeth can help you get the sound right when you are practicing.

Practice Listening to Troublesome Consonants

Listen to the following phrases from the interview with Suzanne Stephens. As you listen, circle each word that contains a consonant sound that you need to practice. Then, rewind the tape and repeat each phrase after the speaker, being careful to correctly pronounce words containing the consonant sound you are practicing.

1. I think in our particular area especially here in North Carolina, there are really two that come to mind.

2. First would be growth, residential growth, industrial growth.

3. Most of us live here too. We don't just run our businesses, we also have our homes and our families.

4. There are a lot more businesses than there are government inspectors to go out and inspect.

5. We also want to go boating, and go swimming, and take long hikes in the forest. And, because we as individuals have to live here as well as work here, I believe that businesses are going to become more and more conscious of how we treat the environment.

Practice Pronouncing Troublesome Consonants

Some students of English find that practicing "tongue twisters," in which a difficult sound appears many times, can help them to learn to pronounce a sound correctly. Following are some tongue twisters containing the sounds covered in this chapter.

1. Little Lila liked to lick luscious lemony lollipops.

2. Rita and Roger ran 'round and 'round the raspberry bush.

3. Red light, green light, right light, left light

4. Thirty thousand thirsty snakes thirstily drank three thousand lakes.

5. Whether the weather is cold, whether the weather is hot, we'll be together whatever the weather, whether we like it or not.

With your classmates, create other tongue twisters that include many words with a sound that is difficult for you.

Communicative Pronunciation Practice

Look at the lists below. Add five words with troublesome consonants that you would like to practice to each list.

/r/ versus /l/	/θ/ versus /ð/
resources	truth
recycling	think
right	ethical
wrong	growth
really	through
live	this
last	these
lazy	whether
believe	together
a lot	worthy

Using ten words from the lists, in any order, give your opinion on the question, "Should businesses be responsible for protecting the environment?" When planning your answer, make a special effort to use words that include the troublesome consonant that you chose to practice in this chapter. Tape record your opinion, or present it in class.

Discussion Skills: Using Words to Your Advantage

People make important judgements about politicians, companies, and other people by the words that they say. For this reason, politicians and companies hire official spokespeople to monitor public opinion about politics and business and to help them to use words so as to change the public's opinion to their advantage. This is called "spinning" a situation. "Spinning" is taking something that might be perceived as negative and presenting it in a way that seems less negative, or even positive.

For example, if a company is caught breaking environmental laws, its spokespeople (sometimes called "spindoctors") will decide how to react officially. They might choose their words carefully to make the company's actions seem like a small mistake, or they might apologize officially, hoping that the public will forgive the company. Sometimes they will even try to find a way to turn the situation to the company's advantage, for example, by showing how the government is stopping it from doing some good thing, such as creating jobs.

For example, instead of a company's responding to a governmental report that the building of a new factory will harm the habitat of an endangered species by saying this:

"Yes, our factory will help to cause the extinction of this bird."

its official spokesperson might say this:

"The building of this factory will bring many benefits to this community, but our opponents value the lives of birds more highly than the quality of life of people."

This statement is not a lie. It encourages people to look at the issue from another point of view. However, as a listener, you must be able to recognize that the information that you are getting is being "spun" or "doctored." You will have to get the facts and make your own decisions.

As companies and politicians have mastered the art of using words to *their* advantage, you too can improve the judgments that people make about you by using words to *your* advantage. For example, you can convince your friends, parents or spouse to agree with your ideas or opinions, and even present yourself favorably in job interviews or discussions at work.

"Spinning" is common and important. However, be sure to use it carefully so that you don't misrepresent the truth or tell a lie.

Listening to How Words Can Be Used to Gain Advantage

Listen again to the interview with Suzanne Stephens about environmental ethics. Notice how she chooses her words carefully to show a positive relationship among business, the environment, and the government. Write down at least three examples of these words and phrases.

_____

_____

_____

Practicing Choosing Words to Gain Advantage

Follow these steps to practice using words to your advantage.

1. Choose one of the following pieces of advice about what should be done to save the environment, and list the positive and negative effects that would occur if people followed this advice.
   - Farmers should not use pesticides.
   - Wilderness areas should be kept free of tourists.
   - Countries should be forced to protect their rainforests.
   - The price of gasoline should be raised to three dollars a gallon.

2. Plan a three- to five-minute statement from the point of view of *someone who supports this action*.

3. Then, plan another three- to five-minute statement from the point of view of *someone who opposes it*.

When planning your statements, remember to choose your words carefully so that the statement makes both sides look positive. Present your statements to your classmates or record it on audio tape or video tape.

4. As you listen to each statement of your classmates', answer the following questions to evaluate how well you and your classmates are able to choose advantageous words.
   a. Were both the supporting and opposing statements equally convincing? If one was more convincing, which one? What was convincing about it?
   b. What advantageous words and phrases did the presenter use to give the statement a positive spin? Did the speaker use any words that have negative connotations? What words with positive connotations could have been used instead?
   c. Did the speaker say anything that misrepresented the truth or tell any lies? How could these untruths be eliminated from the presentation.

Collecting Images from Nature

Sometimes, we forget to think about nature. We are so busy with our day-to-day lives that we do not look around us to see the beauty of our natural environment. For this exercise, collect images or objects from nature that represent something that does the following.

- Makes you feel happy
- Makes you feel nervous
- Reminds you of your childhood
- Looks like a human face
- Reminds you of something positive about yourself
- Reminds you of something negative about yourself
- Reminds you of someone whom you love

Bring these objects to class, and explain your choices to a small group of your classmates. You might want to talk about where you found the objects or images, why you chose them, and how they make you feel.

Investigating the Throw-Away Mentality

Find an artifact (an object that humans use) that represents the throw-away mentality. This artifact could be an actual item, such as a plastic bottle, or an advertisement for goods or a service from a magazine or newspaper. Bring your artifact to class, and be prepared to discuss the following.

1. What it is.

2. What it is used for.

3. Why it represents the idea of a throw-away society.

Self-Evaluation

Use the following checklist to evaluate your work in this chapter. Mark how well you think that you achieved this chapter's goals. Your teacher might also mark the checklist to evaluate your work. For areas marked as Needs Improvement, you should review the appropriate sections of the chapter to be sure that you get the additional practice that you need.

Goal	Excellent	Good	Needs Improvement
1. Listening for context and main ideas	_____	_____	_____
2. Listening for detail	_____	_____	_____
3. Reductions with /t/	_____	_____	_____
4. Asking for clarification	_____	_____	_____
5. Troublesome consonants: /r/, /l/, /θ/, and /ð/	_____	_____	_____
6. Using words to your advantage	_____	_____	_____

Comments

CHAPTER 5
Private Lives, Public Information

—— ✴ ——

Chapter Highlights

▶ Listening for main ideas

▶ Listening for details

▶ Pronouncing can and can't

▶ Expressing anger and frustration

▶ Listening for reasons

▶ Focal stress

▶ Supporting your opinions with reasons

Discussion Questions

Free-write, tape record, or discuss your answers to the following questions with others in your class.

1. What would you do if you told a friend something private and your friend told someone else? Has this ever happened to you? How did you feel? What did you do about it?

2. Do you feel that celebrities, politicians, and other "public people" should expect the media to try to find out and publish information about their private lives? What do you think that the media should be allowed to publish? In your opinion, is there anything that the media should not be allowed to make public?

Introductory Activity: Interpreting a Cartoon

Look at the following cartoon from *The New Yorker*, make sure that you understand the words in the cartoon, and then discuss the questions that follow.

1. What is the main idea of this cartoon? Do you think that the cartoon is funny? Why or why not?

2. What does the cartoon say about the media? Do you think that the cartoon accurately depicts the media in the United States and/or Canada?

Before You Listen: Discussion Questions

Before listening to this conversation, discuss the following questions with others of your classmates.

1. Think of a time when you were angry with a friend. What made you angry? Do you show anger to your friends and family differently than you do to strangers? How?

2. What do you do if you are having difficulty with a class in school? Do you ask a teacher for help? A friend? Someone else? How does having difficulty with a class make you feel?

Global Listening: Main Ideas

🔲 Read the following statements. Then, listen to the recording of an angry conversation between two roommates, Sylvia and Anne. As you listen, mark each of the statements as true or false.

1. Anne is angry with Sylvia.	True	False
2. Sylvia thinks that her math grade should be private.	True	False
3. Anne was trying to help Sylvia.	True	False
4. Margie will come over to help Sylvia study.	True	False

Closer Listening: Details

🔲 Listen to the conversation again. This time, make notes of the answers to the following questions.

1. What is Sylvia's problem?

2. Why is Sylvia angry with Anne?

3. How did Anne try to help Sylvia? Why?

4. How does Sylvia decide to solve her problem with her math class?

After You Listen: Discussion Questions

Discuss the following questions with others in your class.

1. Do you believe that Anne was right or wrong to tell Margie about Sylvia's math class? Why?

2. How do you think that Sylvia feels about the difficulty she has with her class? How do you know?

3. What gestures and facial expressions do you think that Sylvia and Anne are making as they argue?

4. At the end of the conversation, what does Anne mean when she says she's "learned her lesson"?

Cultural Notes: Privacy

In general, most Americans and Canadians are very protective of many parts of their private lives and are reluctant to share information about money, health, and age with others. However, pop culture and the media, especially in the United States, are always reporting details about the lives of celebrities, politicians, and other well-known people. Even some average citizens do not seem to be embarrassed to share on TV talk shows the details of their personal relationships.

Different cultures think of privacy in different ways. Culture defines both the kind of information that is considered to be private as well as the situations in which people are willing (or forced) to share information that is considered personal. Knowing how a culture or an individual feels about personal privacy can help you to know what questions might be considered impolite and can help you to avoid embarrassment.

Read the following list of topics that people talk about. In the first column, write the word "public" or "private" to show whether you think a topic is public or private. In the second and third columns, write "public" or "private" to show what most people think of these topics in your culture and in at least one other culture that you are familiar with. Why do you think that people consider these topics to be private or public?

Topics	You	Your Culture	Other Culture: _____
Family			
Health			
Grades and school work			
Salary			
Prices of possessions			
Food			
Political party membership			
Opinions about neighboring countries and borders			
Pregnancy			
Age			
Talents and abilities			
Social status and class			
Religious beliefs			

Pronunciation

Can and Can't

In most dialects of North American English, these two simple English words—*can* and *can't*—can be very difficult to understand when they are spoken in a sentence. This is because the rules of pronunciation and sentence stress cause these words to sound different when pronounced in a sentence than when they are pronounced alone.

Three rules affect the pronunciation of *can* and *can't.*

1. A /t/ after an /n/ is often not pronounced. (For more information, review reductions with /t/ in Chapter 4.)

2. A function word is unstressed unless it is emphasized to change the meaning of the sentence. (For more about this rule, see the "Focal Stress" box later in this chapter.)

3. The vowel sound in a stressed word is full, while the vowel sound in an unstressed word is reduced to /ə/.

According to these rules, *can't* is usually pronounced /kæn/ because it is a stressed word with a full vowel and a reduced /t/. *Can* is pronounced /kən/ because it is an unstressed word with a reduced vowel. These rules show that *can't* often sounds like *can* and *can* sounds something like *kun.* No wonder it is confusing! Even native speakers get confused. If that happens, just ask, "Did you say *can* or *cannot?*"

Practice Listening to Can and Can't

Listen to the following sentences and phrases from Sylvia and Anne's conversation, which you just heard. As you hear each sentence or phrase, circle whether the speaker says can or can't.

1. I can/can't believe you told Margie I'm failing my math class!

2. You know I can/can't stand it!

3. We can/can't order a pizza.

4. Can/Can't you understand?

5. I just want to be sure you can/can't pass your class.

6. I can/can't call her and tell her it's off.

7. It's my responsibility to help out if I can/can't.

8. I can/can't handle it.

Practice Pronouncing Can and Can't

To practice pronouncing can and can't, read this paragraph and then complete each of the following blanks with either the word "can" or "can't." Then reread the paragraph aloud to a partner, your teacher, or on audio tape.

> Whenever I meet new people, I _____ get over the fear that I will ask a question about something that they feel is private and personal. I know that there are many things I _____ talk about with them, but I _____ always think of the right questions. I know that you _____ offend people by asking the wrong question, so I sometimes get so tongue-tied I _____ speak. My friend Lucy _____ talk about anything with anybody. She _____ always think of something to say and _____ understand why I get so nervous. She says I _____ solve my problem unless I think more about being interested in what I _____ learn about someone and not worry so much about what I _____ and _____ say.

Communicative Pronunciation Practice: Sharing Secrets

Think of five secrets that a friend might share with you. Write these secrets in the first column of the following chart. Then, in the second column, write the names of people with whom you probably *can* share the secret. In the third column, write the names of people with whom you *can't* share the secret. Remember, for some secrets you can't tell anyone and for others you can tell everyone.

Secret	People You Can Tell	People You Can't Tell
Example: I'm going to break up with my girlfriend.	Your roommate, who doesn't know your friend	The girlfriend

After completing your chart, tell your classmates about your decisions. Be sure to pronounce can and can't correctly. Discuss with your classmates your choices and their possible consequences. Who made the best decisions? Who made the worst?

TALK It Through!

Conversational Skills: Expressing Anger and Frustration

How can you know if a North American is angry or frustrated with you? And if you are upset, how can you express this in a way that is clear and that doesn't make the situation worse? Phrases for expressing anger vary according to formality and levels of directness. Usually, when North Americans speak with someone whom they don't know or someone of higher status (for example, a boss or professor), they use formal, indirect language and include the person's formal title or name. For example:

Excuse me, Dr. Jones, but it upsets me when … .

I don't want to offend you, Ms. Parker, but I'm concerned about … .

I understand, Margaret, but I am very disappointed by … .

I'm sorry, Professor, but I'm uncomfortable with … .

Less formal and more direct language is used to speak with friends, family, or people whom one knows well. For example:

It's frustrating when … .

It bothers me when … .

I don't like it when … .

It kind of bugs me when ... .

It really annoys me when ... .

I can't stand it when ... .

When you are a part of an angry conversation, you might need to interrupt the person with whom you are arguing in order to express an opinion, to express agreement or disagreement, or to apologize. This is not always easy, especially if the person is very emotional and perhaps is not listening to you. Phrases for interrupting vary in politeness. For example:

More polite:	I'm sorry to interrupt, but . . . .
	I hate to interrupt, but ... .
	I don't want to interrupt, but ... .
	Pardon my interruption, but ... .
Less polite:	Hold on!
	Wait a minute!
	Hey!

Of course, sometimes a person can express anger by saying nothing at all. Instead of complaining, an angry or frustrated person might simply stop talking to you. This is called the "silent treatment." What can you do if someone is giving you the silent treatment?

Listening to the Language

Listen again to the argument between Sylvia and Anne. They use many phrases to express anger and to interrupt one another. As you listen to the conversation, list in the following chart phrases for expressing anger and phrases for interrupting.

Phrases for Expressing Anger	Phrases for Interrupting

Role-Play Situations for Angry Situations

Practice expressing anger and frustration constructively. Role-play one of the following scenes with a partner. Use the phrases that you read about previously for interrupting and for expressing anger and frustration.

Scene A: Neighbor One is playing loud rock music from his or her stereo very late on a weeknight. Neighbor Two is in the apartment next door, studying for an exam.

Neighbor One: You are having a small party with some friends from out of town, and you think that it is your right to play your stereo as you like. Refuse to turn it down.

Neighbor Two: The loudness of the music is really bothering you. You can't study, and you threaten to call the police.

Scene B: A customer is complaining to a dry cleaner about the way his or her shirt was laundered.

Customer: You claim that the dry cleaner shrunk your favorite shirt and that it's ruined. You insist that the dry cleaner pay for it.

Dry Cleaner: You have asked the customer for a receipt and he or she does not have one. You say that you will not pay because you do not know if your store is responsible for the damage.

Scene C: Two friends agree to meet each other at the movie theater to watch the latest box-office hit.

Friend One: You arrived on time and have been waiting for half an hour. The movie, which you really wanted to see, has started and you are very frustrated and angry with your friend because he or she is always late, even when it is important to be on time.

Friend Two: You got stuck in traffic and couldn't find a parking space. You are not really concerned because you didn't really want to see the movie.

If you have ever shopped in a supermarket, convenience store, or gas station, you have probably seen tabloid papers reporting stories about celebrities, other people, and events which are almost unbelievable. Some people like to read these stories because they are entertaining. Some people might say that the newspapers have a right to print anything that they want and that famous people need to have their pictures and stories about them in the tabloids or they will not be famous anymore. Other people believe that the tabloids tell lies, spread rumors, and give away information that should be kept private. These people believe that even famous people have a right to private lives. We asked four people in New Jersey to tell us what they think about these tabloid magazines.

Before You Listen: Reading about Freedom of the Press

Read the following information about freedom of the press, and discuss the questions that follow.

Freedom of the Press

The Constitution of the United States and an important court decision in Canada give the press—that is newspaper, TV, and radio news organizations, and so on—in these countries the right to publish any information that they can prove is true. Also, these news organizations are separate from the government and cannot be controlled by the government. The people who wrote the U.S. Constitution wanted the press to be able to check on the government, businesses, and community leaders to be sure that they are telling the truth and acting fairly.

There are many good things about the free press, but some journalists, magazines, and TV shows abuse this right. They publish personal information, gossip, and embarrassing photographs about celebrities and governmental leaders, and they sometimes print stories that are not true. Some people believe that laws should be passed to restrict how much personal information the press can publish. This would protect people's privacy, but it would damage the freedom of the press.

To some people, freedom of the press is one of the most important ideas in U.S. society because it ensures that people can get information from independent sources and make judgments about what is true and false for themselves. These people say that even though some journalists misuse the right to a free press, it so important to have a free press that we should not pass laws controlling what can be published.

Comprehension Questions

1. What is "freedom of the press"?

2. How do some journalists abuse the right to a free press?

3. What are some of the advantages of having a free press that is not controlled by the government? What are some of the disadvantages?

Vocabulary Development

The people who give their opinions in the upcoming taped interview use vocabulary that makes the reasons that they give for their opinions more emphatic and persuasive. In the following sentences, the underlined words and phrases come from the interviews that you will hear. Each word or phrase fits into one of the following four categories. Use the context of the sentences to match each word or phrase to the correct category.

a. To look for negative information about someone
b. To read something briefly, looking only at what catches your eye
c. Untrue or unprovable
d. What some tabloids might do to sell more newspapers

____ 1. I didn't know the correct answer, so *I made one up.*

____ 2. I didn't read the whole story. I just *glanced at it.*

____ 3. I don't think reporters should *dig into somebody's personal background* looking for mistakes that the person made in the past.

____ 4. I usually don't read magazines, but sometimes *I'll flip through them.*

____ 5. I don't think that photograph is real; it looks *phony.*

____ 6. Some tabloid photographers and writers *assume that people's personal lives are wide open for speculation and gossip.*

____ 7. Her story isn't completely untrue, but she *embellished* it by adding untrue details.

____ 8. That story about our neighbor is just *gossip,* and no one knows if it's true.

____ 9. If reporters didn't *dig up dirt* about politicians, we might never learn which politicians are dishonest.

____ 10. The story was full of *innuendo,* but it never directly said that the man was a thief.

____ 11. If you say anything to hurt her reputation, she might sue you for *slander.*

____ 12. When reporters *go above and beyond the calls of decency,* I think they shouldn't be allowed to publish their reports because the reports might offend people.

____ 13. Tabloids think *juicy* headlines make people buy the paper to read the story inside.

Global Listening: Main Ideas

Listen to four people answer questions about tabloid magazines. As you listen, circle yes or no in the second column of the following chart to show each person's answer to these questions.

Question	Answer		Reason for the Answer
1. Do you read tabloids?			
Angelo	Yes	No	
Dave	Yes	No	
Mary Jane	Yes	No	
Katie	Yes	No	
2. Do you think that tabloids should be stopped from publishing private information about celebrities?			
Angelo	Yes	No	
Dave	Yes	No	
Mary Jane	Yes	No	
Katie	Yes	No	

Closer Listening: Listening for Reasons

The people who answer the questions in this survey give reasons for each opinion that they express. Listen to the recording a second time. This time use the third column in the previous chart to write the letter of the reason that each person gives.

Reasons for Reading/Not Reading Tabloids

a. They are entertaining.
b. There is no news in them.
c. I'm interested in celebrities.
d. It is hurtful to people.

Reasons for Controlling/Not Controlling Tabloids

e. Celebrities have a right to privacy, too.
f. No one believes tabloids anyway.
g. Tabloids should concentrate on facts.
h. Anyone who believes tabloids is more foolish than the tabloid writer.

Pronunciation

Focal Stress

In Chapter 2, you learned about how the patterns of stressed syllables and stressed content words give the English language its rhythm. The way words that are stressed, however, can also affect the meaning of sentences and phrases. Speakers of English will often give a word extra stress to focus on one word in a thought group. Usually this is the last word in the thought group, but sometimes another word is stressed to emphasize only that one word in the thought group. Consider the following sentence:

> I'm thinking about buying a tabloid.

If you changed the focal stress in the following ways, you could communicate several different meanings. Try stressing the different words as you read these sentences. Can you "sense" the difference in meaning?

> I'm thinking about buying a TABloid. (I am trying to decide if I want to buy a tabloid.)

> I'm thinking about BUYing a tabloid. (I want to buy a tabloid and not read someone else's.)

> I'm THINKing about buying a tabloid. (I haven't decided yet. I'm just thinking.)

> I'M thinking about buying a tabloid. (You aren't thinking about it, but I am!)

Focal stress is used to do the following.

Emphasize new information in a sentence. The last content word in a sentence usually contains the newest information. In a conversation, though, sometimes the new information is in a different place. For example:

> A: Did Tiffany buy a CAR?

> B: Yes, she bought a RED car.

Emphasize agreement or disagreement with another's opinion. This often happens in discussions and disagreements when someone emphasizes a difference of opinion. For example:

> A: I don't that think you told me anything PRIvate.

> B: Well, I DO think that information is private.

Emphasize a word or idea that the speaker feels strongly about. This can happen with any word, but it often happens with words such as *not, never, very,* and *completely.*

> It was comPLETEly inappropriate to tell him.

> I'm NEVER going to tell you a secret again.

Practice Predicting Focal Stress

The following four excerpts are from the interviews about tabloids. For each thought group, underline the word that you think will receive focal stress. Hint: On each line, only one word receives focal stress.

Excerpt #1: **The standard pattern, emphasizing new information**
There's really nothing in those tabloids
that interests me
as far as news.

Excerpt #2: **Emphasizing an idea that the speaker feels strongly about**
I find some of the stuff
is totally not believable.

Excerpt #3: **Emphasizing agreement**
I do think they should have limits
and I think they do go too far.

Excerpt #4: **Emphasizing an idea that the speaker feels strongly about**
Ninety percent of what's in there isn't factual
and it's, it's gossip
and its innuendo
and it's, it's slander!

Practice Listening to Focal Stress

Next, listen again to the recording, circling the words that really do receive focal stress. Compare your answers with your classmates'.

1. Were your predictions correct?

2. If your predictions differ from what you heard, try reading the excerpt with the focal stress used in the recording. Then try reading the excerpt with the focal stress that you predicted.

3. As a class, decide if the difference in focal stress changes the meaning of the excerpt.

Practice Pronouncing Focal Stress

With a partner, practice reading the following dialog. Be careful to pronounce the focal stress correctly. When you feel comfortable reading the dialog, perform it for your class or record it on audio tape.

A: Did you hear the NEWS about ROB SIMon?

B: Rob Simon the famous SINGer?

A: Yeah! Did you know he wants to MARRY a MONkey?

B: A MONkey? Where did you hear THAT?

A: It was in *The Daily RUmor.*

B: You call THAT the news? I NEVer believe THAT trash!

Communicative Pronunciation Practice

Spreading Rumors

Practice focal stress that emphasizes new information, contrasting opinions, and important ideas by writing "rumor" dialogs. In these dialogs, imitate the way that rumors spread. The first speaker starts a rumor. As each speaker hears the rumor, he or she changes it a little bit. For example:

A: I heard that the mayor bought a new CAR.

B: The mayor bought an exPENsive car.

C: The mayor's expensive CAR was bought with the CITY's money.

D: The mayor STOLE city money to buy a CAR.

E: The mayor didn't STEAL the money. He bought the car with his OWN money!

F: What a TERRible rumor!

Work in a group of three or more students to write your rumor dialog. Underline the words that should receive focal stress, and have your teacher check your work. Then practice your dialog, and perform it for the class, being sure to use correct focal stress.

TALK It Through!

Discussion Skills: Giving Reasons to Support Your Opinions

Whether a discussion takes place in business, academia, or among friends, English speakers often express strong opinions. They do this not to argue with one another but because they are able to explore different ideas about a topic together from different viewpoints. Because the goal of a discussion is to examine the many different sides of a topic, question, or problem, it is important that participants in the discussion give logical and valid reasons to support their opinions. Giving reasons to support an opinion can also help make an opinion more interesting, credible, and persuasive to a listener.

Clearly expressing an opinion and the reasons for it in a discussion can be challenging, especially if the discussion is fast-paced. The following hints and strategies might help you.

- Whenever possible, think ahead of time about the topic that you will be discussing. Think about your reasons, and perhaps even make notes of them, so that you will be better prepared to state your reasons during the discussion.
- After expressing your opinion, use phrases such as *I mean, I think, such as, like, because,* and *for example,* and then follow with your reasons.
- When you are just learning to express opinions and the reasons that support them, it can help to hear others express their own opinions and reasons for them. You can ask people to do this by using phrases such as, *Why do you feel this way?* or *Can you give me an example?* or simply *What's your reason for saying that?*
- If you need a little time to think, you can tell the group by saying *I need a moment to think about this,* or *Could you come back to me? I'll give you my reasons in a minute.*

Identifying Reasons That Support Opinions

In the interviews about tabloids that you listened to earlier in this chapter, people are asked their opinions about whether the tabloids go too far in reporting people's private lives. Read the four responses, or listen to the recording again. Rank the reasons given for each opinion from 1 to 4. Put a 1 next to the reason that is most interesting, credible, and persuasive and a 4 next to the reason that is least effective. Then, discuss your choices with your classmates.

Question: Do you think that (the tabloids) should be more respectful of peoples' privacy? Should they stop reporting celebrity scandals?

_____ **Opinion #1:** Well, you gotta figure half the stuff in there is phony or made up or maybe embellished anyway. So anyone that actually believes what's in there is probably a bigger fool than, uh, the people that write it.

_____ **Opinion #2:** Aah, sure, but I mean, you know, you don't really believe it anyway, so … .

_____ **Opinion #3:** I do think they should stop and have limits, and I think they do go too far like, … if somebody has AIDS or something like that. They have no right to reveal that to the public unless the person wants to make that known. I think celebrities have the right to , too.

_____ **Opinion #4:** I think that first of all they need to concentrate on being factual. I mean it's, it's true that there's lot of amazing and different types of things that happen in this country that are factual, and I think that you need to stick to that. And, just because someone is a celebrity or is a well-known personality, that, it doesn't mean that their personal life is wide open for speculation and gossip, and I just think that they are too interested in making things juicy and interesting they have gotten so completely far away from the facts. That is, it's time to stop.

Using Facts and Examples to Support Your Opinion

Hold a discussion with others in your class in which you try to answer the question asked in the listening: "Do the tabloids and other sensational media such as TV talk shows go too far?" Follow these steps to plan and conduct your discussion.

1. Gather three or more examples of tabloid media. For example, you could watch a video tape of a TV talk show, visit Internet sites that specialize in gossip, or look at examples of tabloid newspapers and magazines.

2. Read or watch the examples that you chose to help form your opinion on this issue. For example, do you think that these media are just entertainment that give famous people, and people who want to be famous, the attention that they want and need. Do you think that the stories shown in these examples are invasions of people's privacy and should be stopped? Or, do you have a different opinion?

3. Look at your example videos or publications again. This time, make notes of stories, images, or other items that support your opinion.

4. Discuss with your classmates the question about whether sensational TV talk shows and tabloid magazines go too far. Remember that in North American classroom discussions, you are trying to explore a problem from many perspectives and not necessarily trying to get or force others to agree with you.

FURTHER PRACTICE

Using the Internet

Privacy on the Internet

Now that the Internet is being used for business, many people are concerned about the security of their personal information on-line, such as e-mail addresses, credit card numbers, and other personal information. To learn more about Internet privacy, visit one or more of the following sites and then report to your class on what you discovered.

www.computerprivacy.org
www.privacy.nb.ca
www.privacy.org
www.privacyalliance.org

Opinions about Privacy

Many people want to keep personal information private, but companies want this information, such as medical records, financial information, or even telephone numbers and e-mail and home addresses. Companies use this information to decide if a person might be interested in their products and to send advertisements or call the person at home to make special offers. Interview someone to find out whether he or she is bothered by such things as telephone solicitation, junk mail, and possible privacy violations. If you need to review how to do an interview, refer to Chapter 3, page 46.

Self-Evaluation

Use the following checklist to evaluate your work in this chapter. Mark how well you think that you have achieved this chapter's goals. Your teacher might also mark the checklist to evaluate your work. For areas marked as Needs Improvement, you should reread or relisten to the appropriate sections of the chapter to be sure that you get the additional practice that you need.

Goal	Excellent	Good	Needs Improvement
1. Listening for main ideas	_____	_____	_____
2. Listening for details	_____	_____	_____
3. Pronouncing *can* and *can't*	_____	_____	_____
4. Expressing anger and frustration	_____	_____	_____
5. Listening for reasons	_____	_____	_____
6. Focal stress	_____	_____	_____
7. Supporting your opinions with reasons	_____	_____	_____

Comments

CHAPTER 6
Transportation Troubles

Chapter Highlights

▶ Listening to main ideas and details

▶ Consonant clusters

▶ Giving directions

▶ Making inferences

▶ Linking

▶ Persuasion

Discussion Questions

Free write, tape record, or discuss your answers to these questions with others in your class.

1. As the world's urban population continues to grow, and as more and more of this population choose to drive cars to work, traffic is quickly becoming one of the biggest problems in people's everyday lives. What are some of the solutions to transportation problems that you have heard of or that you can think of?

2. All of us have to figure out how we are going to get from our homes to work, school, and other activities, such as a movie, a friend's house, and so on. What transportation issues do you face in your everyday life?

Introductory Activity: Making Predictions from Data in a Table

As more and more people on the planet drive cars, the amount of carbon dioxide, or CO_2, in our atmosphere also increases. Carbon dioxide is an odorless, colorless gas that is very important to the life-sustaining processes on Earth. However, many scientists believe that too much carbon dioxide can cause many environmental problems, such as global warming.

Study the following table, which shows predictions about how cars and traffic might affect our atmosphere in the future. Then discuss the questions that follow with others in your class.

Cars and Air Quality

Current and Future Scenarios	Change in the Increase in CO_2 in Our Atmosphere	
	Over 20 Years	Over 40 Years
Current Situation A 1.5% increase per year in the number of miles that people travel in their private cars.	+35%	+80%
Possible Solution Reduce motor vehicle travel by 20% through public transportation, carpooling, and so on.	−5% to −10%	−10% to −20%
Possible Solution Make cars and trucks use fuel 1.5% more economically per year.	−10% to −20%	−30% to −40%
Possible Solution Increase the cost of petroleum by 3% per year.	−10% to −20%	−30% to −40%

Data from *Public Roads* (1998) Department of Transportation.

Discussion Questions

1. What does this table predict for the future of Earth's atmosphere if we don't change how we use transportation? What does the table suggest can be done to reduce this problem?

2. The table suggests several solutions for reducing pollution from automobiles and other motor vehicles. Which of these do you believe will be easiest for human beings around the world to implement? Which will be the most difficult? Why?

3. Pollution is just one transportation problem that must be solved now and in the future. Make a list of other problems related to transportation that you are aware of.

Before You Listen: Using Maps

Mark is new in town and doesn't know his way around very well. He is at the train station and needs to get to his friend Hilary's house. Look at the following map, and suggest two ways that Mark can get to Hilary's place from the train station.

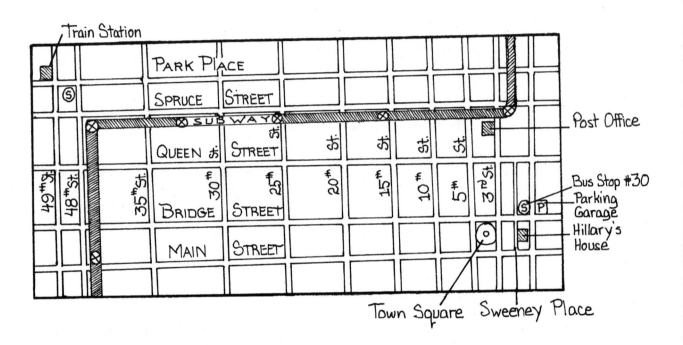

Suggestion 1:_____

Suggestion 2:_____

Global Listening: Main Idas

Listen to the dialog, and answer the following questions.

1. Mark is late for dinner for several reasons. What are they?

   _____

   _____

2. What are three forms of public transportation mentioned in the dialog?

   _____

   _____

   _____

3. What form of transportation does Mark finally decide to take?

   _____

Closer Listening: Details

Listen to the dialog again. Hilary and Mark discuss several ways for Mark to get from the train station to Hilary's house. As you listen, in the following chart, write down the problems with taking a bus, the subway, or a taxi to get to Hilary's house.

Transportation Option	Problems
Bus	
Subway	
Taxi	

Consonant Clusters

Consonant clusters are groups of consonants pronounced together with no vowel between them. For some English learners, consonant clusters can be very difficult because they do not occur in every language. Up to three consonants can cluster at the beginning of a word, and up to four can appear in the middle or at the end of a word. For example, the word "strengths" has three consonant sounds at the beginning and four consonant sounds at the end:

strengths /strɛŋkθs/

Mistakes to Watch For

People who speak languages that do not have consonant clusters will often insert a vowel sound before the cluster or between the consonants in the cluster to make the cluster easy to say. If for the word "strengths" you say "/ɛstrɛŋkθsɛ/" or "/sɛtɛrɛŋkɛθs/," your listener might misunderstand you.

Consonant clusters consist of two or more of the following sounds:

/l/, /r/, /s/, /w/, /b/, /p/, /d/, /g/, /f/, /t/, /k/, /θ/

To help you to pronounce these consonant clusters, try pronouncing a word that has the cluster by adding one consonant at a time. For example, if you have difficulty pronouncing the word *scream* /skriym/, first practice saying *ream*, then *cream*, and finally *scream*. You can do the same with clusters at the ends of words. When practicing the word *world* /wɛrld/, first say *were*, then *whirl*, and then *world*. This will take practice, but it can help you to train your mouth to say these challenging sounds!

When a consonant cluster is in the middle of a word, connect the first consonant(s) to the vowel in front of the cluster and then connect the last consonant(s) to the vowel that follows the cluster. For example, practice pronouncing the word

extreme   /əkstriym/

by dividing the consonants between the two syllables:

/əks-triym/.

By doing this, you have to pronounce only two small clusters instead of one large cluster with four consonants. Each time that you practice, reduce the pause between the two syllables until you are able to pronounce the cluster easily.

Practice Listening to Consonant Clusters

Listen to the following phrases from the dialog that you just heard. Each phrase contains consonant clusters in the beginning, middle, or end of words. As you listen, circle each consonant cluster that you can identify. Remember that consonant clusters are identified by sound and not spelling.

1. Where in the world are you?
2. I missed the express train.
3. On Park Place just across the street from Alex's.
4. In front of the parking garage on the corner of Second and Bridge.
5. It's rush hour, and there's a lot of construction, so traffic is gonna be tight on Queen Street.
6. There's one about two blocks from you on 48th and Spruce.

Now, practice pronouncing each word in these sentences that contains a consonant cluster. When you feel that you are able to pronounce these clusters well, rewind the tape and repeat the sentences after the speaker.

Practice Pronouncing Consonant Clusters

To practice pronouncing consonant clusters that have three or more sounds, list in the following chart all of the words that you can think of that have these clusters. These clusters are found at the beginning of words and in the middle of words.

	Beginning of Words	Middle of Words (often with /k/)
/str/	*stretch*	*extreme*
/spr/		
/skw/		
/spl/		
/skr/		

The clusters in the following chart are found at the end of words. Many words with these clusters are in plural nouns and past tense verbs. To review the pronunciation of –s and –ed endings, see Chapter 3. To practice pronouncing these consonant clusters, list in the following chart all of the words that you can think of that have them.

	End of Words
/rdgd/	*charged*
/rts/	
/rns/	
/rld/	
/lfθs/	
/ŋkt/	
/ŋks/	
/rsts/	
/ksθs/	

Communicative Pronunciation Practice

To practice pronunciation of consonant clusters, work with a group of your classmates to make up a story about Trent's terrible day. Follow these steps.

1. Following is a list of misfortunes that Trent suffered during his bad day. Add to the list your own ideas about Trent's bad luck on this day. Include as many words with consonant clusters as you can.

Trent had a very bad day. He

- couldn't find free parking and had to park in an expensive garage.
- spilled his drink on his sweater.
- tripped and stubbed his toe three times.
- locked his keys and driver's license in his truck.
- forgot his textbook and homework for class.
- lost the present that he planned to give his girlfriend.
- got a poor grade and critical comments on his essay in English class.
- broke his pen and got black ink on his white shirt.

_____

_____

_____

_____

_____

_____

2. The class divides into two groups. One group looks at the map on page 96, and the other looks at the list of Trent's misfortunes. Both groups then work together to make up a story about Trent's unlucky day. The students looking at the map should give Trent's location, and the students looking at the list should add an event. For example:

Group A	**Group B**
Trent was driving down Fifth Street...	and he couldn't find free parking and had to park in an expensive garage.

3. If you have access to a tape recorder, record your group's story. When finished, listen to the audio tape to hear how successfully you pronounced the consonant clusters in the story.

Conversational Skills: Giving Directions

To give directions, follow these three steps.

1. Start by stating where the directions are beginning (the point of origin) and where they will end (the point of destination). For example:

   To get to my house from the train station, ...

   To get to the university from here, ...

   If you are at the art museum and you are going to the shopping mall, ...

2. Next, give the directions to the destination. Include signposts or other markers, such as buildings, that are along the way. Organize the markers by using connector words such as *first, next, after that,* and *finally.* Use verbs of motion and other common directional phrases such as *go, travel, veer, turn, reach, intersect, hang a left,* and *bear right.*

Directions are given in the *simple present tense* or the *future tense.*

Present Tense

> First, you go down Market Street for about three blocks. The art museum is on your left. When you reach 12th Street, take a right. After that, go two blocks. Hang a left on Pine, and my apartment is in the third building on the right: 1320 Pine Street, apartment 503.

Future Tense

> First, you're going to go down Market Street until you see the art museum on your left. As soon as you pass the art museum, you're going to take a right on 12th. You'll go two blocks on 12th to where it intersects with Pine Street. Finally, take a left on Pine and my apartment building will be on your right: 1320 Pine Street, apartment 503.

Note: For street names, the word "street" is often dropped when directions are given. 12th Street can be referred to as 12th, Pine Street as Pine, and so on.

3. Finally, use some words of encouragement when you have finished giving the directions. For example:

   You won't have any problem finding it!

   It's easy!   It's a piece of cake!

   Good luck!   You can't miss it!

   Give me a call if you get lost.

Listening to the Language

📼 Rewind the tape and listen to the dialog again. Focus on what Hilary says as she explains the directions that Mark should take if he takes the subway to get to her house.

1. How does she introduce the directions?

2. Does she use present tense or future tense when she gives the directions?

3. What does she say to encourage Mark?

Gathering Information from Maps

Imagine that the following is a map of the area that you live in. Study the map and then answer the questions that follow. You might want to do similar activities with a map of the community in which you live.

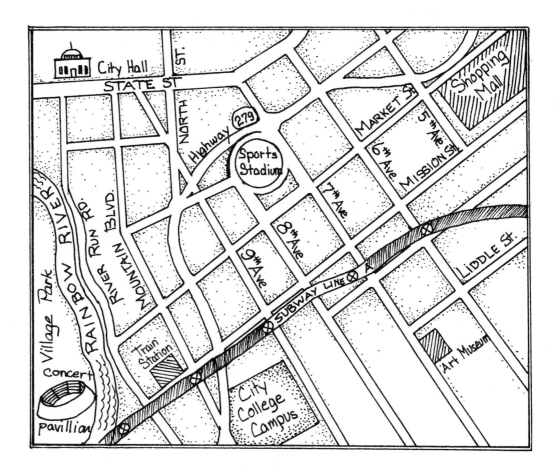

Discussion Questions

Answer the following questions with a partner or on audio tape. As you answer, remember to follow the previous three steps for giving directions.

1. Imagine that you work at the shopping mall and you must get to the city college as soon as possible after work. You know that you will be traveling during rush hour. Would you use rail, subway, bus, bike, or taxi to get from the shopping mall to the college? Why?

2. Imagine that you have to describe the city shown on the map to a partner, someone who is visiting for the first time. Tell your partner some general information about the city, advise him or her to see one of the city's major attractions, and give directions for getting there from the train station.

3. Choose two locations on the map. Tell your partner one location but keep the other a secret. Give your partner directions from the first location to the second. If your partner reaches the second location based on your directions, you will know that you did a good job. If your partner reaches a different destination, try to determine how the miscommunication occurred. Ask your teacher for help if necessary.

LISTENING TWO ▶ Mass Transit

In Los Angeles, the number of cars will soon equal the number of people who live there, adding to the city's already severe traffic and air pollution problems. For this reason, the Los Angeles Metropolitan Transportation Authority, also called the MTA, is working hard to get 15% to 20% of the people who currently drive to work every day to leave their cars at home and use public transportation to commute to work. Jim Delalosa and Ed Scannell are with the MTA. In this interview, we spoke to Ed and Jim and asked them what reasons people give for not using public transportation.

Before You Listen: Making Predictions

To reach its goal, the MTA needs to understand why many commuters prefer to drive their cars through traffic rather than take the Metro or light rail system. In your opinion, what are the advantages and disadvantages of driving versus taking the Metro or light rail system? Write your answers in the following chart.

	Advantages	Disadvantages
Driving your own car to work		
Taking the metro or light rail		

If you had to choose between taking your car to work or taking the train, which would you choose? Why?

Global Listening: Main Ideas

As you listen to this interview, list in the following chart both the positive and negative things that the speakers mention about taking public transportation.

Positive Things about Mass Transit   Negative Things about Mass Transit

_____   _____

_____   _____

_____   _____

Closer Listening: Making Inferences

An MTA market survey found that most people base their decision about what form of transportation to take to work on the following factors: time, reliability, and safety. Listen to the tape again, and for each of these factors write down what the MTA spokesman, Ed Scannell, suggests commuter concerns are and how the MTA plans to solve each.

	Commuter Concerns	MTA's Solution
Time		
Reliability		
Safety		

Cultural Notes: Personal Space

Cultural attitudes about personal space affect our daily decisions, for example whether to take a train or drive a car. Personal space also can affect communication with other people. For example, in some cultures that give low value to personal space, people do not need or expect a great amount of private personal space. In these cultures, people often prefer to be physically close to one another in their homes, at work, during conversations, and even when they are riding public transportation. They often stand close together and might even touch each other while talking.

In cultures that place a high value on personal space, people need a great amount of personal or private space to feel comfortable. In their homes, they prefer to spend time in their "own" rooms, and at work they prefer their "own" offices. In addition, they often dislike public transportation because it forces them to sit close to other people when they would much prefer to be in the private world of their "own" car. In these cultures, people stand some distance apart and rarely touch each other while talking.

Listen to the tape again, and discuss the following questions with others in your class. Use information from the listening to support your answers.

1. Do MTA officials feel that the people of Los Angeles give a high or low value to personal space?

2. How does this cultural value affect the decisions that people make about whether to take their own cars or public transportation? How does the personal space value in your culture affect your daily decisions and communication?

3. What miscommunications might occur if a person from a culture that highly values personal space was talking to a person from a culture that places low value on personal space?

Pronunciation

Linking

Words are sometimes pronounced differently in sentences and phrases than they are when pronounced as a single word. One change that often happens when people speak quickly is *linking*. Linking means that the last sound or sounds of one word are blended together with the first sound or sounds of the next word in the thought group. Several kinds of linking are possible.

Same Consonant Linking

Same consonant linking happens when one word ends with the same consonant sound that the next word begins with. The sound is usually pronounced only once. The two words might sound as though they are one word. For example:

You need to fig*ht t*o get a seat during rush hour.

I'm satisfied with the bu*s s*ervice in my city.

Consonant to Consonant Linking

When a word ends with a /p/, /b/, /t/, /d/, /k/, or /g/ sound, and the next word begins with any consonant, the two words are linked in consonant to consonant linking. The two consonants are pronounced almost simultaneously. The first consonant in the pair might sound as though it isn't pronounced. It might even sound as though it is a part of the second word. For example:

Do you have the righ*t s*chedule?

She decide*d t*o ta*ke th*e train.

Consonant to Vowel Linking

When the first word ends with a consonant and the second word begins with a vowel, the words are linked in consonant to vowel linking. One of the sounds might seem to move to the other word, or the two words might sound as though they are one. For example:

I accepted hi*s e*xcuse for being late.

Can you hel*p u*s plan our trip?

This type of linking can be used as a strategy for pronouncing ending consonant clusters. For example:

He walke*d o*ut of the meeting.

What in the worl*d a*re you doing?

Vowel to Vowel Linking

When a word ends with a vowel and the next word begins with a vowel, the two words are linked in vowel to vowel linking.[1]

I'd prefer to drive m_y o_wn car.

I dr_ew a_ map for you in bl_ue i_nk.

Two important rules apply to linking.

1. When predicting linking, consider the *sounds* that begin and end words and not the *letters* the words are spelled with.

2. Linking occurs only within a thought group. Do not try to link words across phrases. In the sentence, "If you lose the map, everyone will get lost," the words *map* and *everyone* would not be linked because they are not part of the same thought group.

[1]Remember that the vowel sounds /ɪ/, /ɛ/, /æ/, /ʊ/, and /ə/ do not occur at the ends of words.

Practice Predicting Linking

The interview that you just heard contains many examples of linking. Read the following excerpt from the interview. Based on what you just learned, mark the words that you believe will be linked.

When I ride to work on the train, I can sit and close my eyes, fall asleep—as long as I don't miss my stop. Or I can read a book, read a magazine. I can listen to the radio. I can do things that otherwise I might not have been able to do driving a car.

Certainly in a car, you can listen to the radio, but you can't read a book, you can't read a magazine, you can't close your eyes and fall asleep. I can do that on the train, and I think that's, for my money, that's the way to spend my time.

Practice Listening to Linking

Now listen to the tape again, and circle the words that really are linked. Compare your answers with your previous predictions. Were your predictions correct? Why or why not? Finally, with a partner, practice reading the segment, imitating the linking patterns.

Practice Linking

A good way to practice your new linking skills is by reading aloud. The following sentences are famous quotations. Read through them and predict which words should be linked. Then, practice reading them aloud with a partner. You might also want to record yourself on audio tape in order to get feedback from your teacher.

1. I know not with what weapons World War Three will be fought, but World War Four will be fought with sticks and stones. —*Albert Einstein*

2. We live in a society dependent on science and technology, in which hardly anyone knows anything about science and technology. —*Carl Sagan*

3. Trouble brings experience and experience brings wisdom. —*Unknown*

4. If we are not ashamed to think it, we should not be afraid to say it. —*Cicero*

5. Half of our life is spent trying to find something to do with the time we have rushed through life trying to save. —*Will Rogers*

Communicative Pronunciation Practice

Imagine that you are planning a one-week vacation to a popular tourist destination in your region and you want to find the best way to get there. Prepare a presentation for your classmates, or record a two- to three-minute tape comparing and contrasting the travel alternatives to your vacation destination. As you prepare your presentation, follow the following steps.

1. Using newspapers, the yellow pages, your local travel agent, and/or the Internet, research the cost and time that it will take to get to your destination by using different forms of transportation. Fill in the following chart with the information that you collect, and answer the questions that follow.

Type of Transportation	Cost	Time to Destination
Private car		
Rental car		
Bus		
Train		
Air		
Other		

    a.   What is the cheapest way to get to your destination?

    b.   What is the most convenient way?

    c.   What is the most scenic way?

    d.   Which way would you choose to travel to your destination? Why?

2. Prepare a two- to three-minute presentation comparing and contrasting the travel alternatives to your travel destination. You do not need to write down everything that you will say. Instead, take notes to remind yourself of the main points that you would like to share with your audience and refer to these when giving your presentation. As you take these notes, mark where text should be linked, based on what you have learned in this chapter.

3. Practice your presentation, linking the words that you have marked in your text as much as possible.

4. Give your presentation to the class, or tape record it for your teacher. Again, as you speak, concentrate on linking the words that you have marked in your notes.

TALK It Through!

Presentation Skills: Persuasion

In Listening Two in this chapter, you heard that the MTA in Los Angeles is trying to *persuade* people to use public transportation. Persuasion is an important skill that people must use every day. We persuade our friends to join us at social events. We persuade store clerks to allow us to exchange a purchase even though we lost the receipt. Advertisers persuade us to use more products and new products. Governmental officials persuade us to support their programs. It is important to understand persuasion so that you not only persuade others but also know when you are being persuaded! Here are some hints to help you.

Remember Your Audience

When you are trying to persuade someone, it is very important that you remember what motivates your audience. The reason that *you* want something might not be the reason that *they* will agree to it. Try to figure out what will make your audience agree with you, and then emphasize that. If you need help with emphasis, review the section in Chapter 5 on page 89.

Use Examples

Examples from your life or from other people's lives can be very persuasive. Make sure that you choose examples that your audience can relate to. If you are trying to convince your 19-year-old roommate to join a sports team, you will probably be more convincing if you use examples from your own life rather than talk about how much your 70-year-old grandfather enjoyed sports when he was your age.

Make Associations with Positive Things

It is easier to persuade people if you can get them to associate your suggestion, plan, or idea with something that they already think is positive. For example, if a teacher can get students to associate doing homework with things that they like, such as having fun or being successful, the students are more likely to be persuaded to do more homework!

Back Up Your Opinions with Facts and Expert Opinions

Remember that only telling someone "I think it is a good idea" is not enough. Use facts and the opinions of recognized experts to support your cause.

Use Body Language and Tone of Voice to Show Enthusiasm

No one will be persuaded if you present your message in a bored voice and slouching posture. Be sure to show your audience that you believe in what you are saying.

Listening to Examples of Persuasion

In the interview regarding the MTA, Ed Scannell tries to persuade people to try public transportation. Listen to the tape again, and answer the following questions.

1. Do you think that Scannell is persuasive? Do you think that someone who hears him speak will try public transportation? Why or why not?

2. What persuasive techniques does Scannell use in this interview?

Giving a Persuasive Presentation

Plan a short presentation in which you try to convince your classmates to do something. If you need to review how to organize a presentation, refer to Chapter 1, page 13.

1. Decide what you will persuade people to do. For example, you could persuade someone to recycle newspapers, ride a bike instead of driving, visit your hometown for vacation, get a pet, watch a movie that you liked, or stop watching TV for a week.

2. Think about your audience, and plan for examples and associations that you can use in your presentation. You might also want to include some persuasive facts and expert opinions if appropriate.

3. Organize your presentation, and plan any visual aids or notes that you will need. Plan to speak for about five minutes.

4. Practice your presentation. Especially practice body language and tone of voice. You might want to video tape this part.

5. Present your persuasive speech in class.

FURTHER PRACTICE

Discussion Skills: Persuasion

Persuasive speech is used not only in presentations or speeches; it is also used in everyday conversations. With a group of classmates, discuss one or more of the following questions. When expressing opinions, use the skills for persuasive speaking that you practiced in this chapter.

Topic #1:   Have you lived in or visited a city where there was a lot of crime? What problems does a lot of crime cause? How are people trying to solve the problem? Are these solutions working?

Topic #2:   Many people believe that the media, especially the film and music industries, are responsible for many of today's social problems, such as divorce, abuse, and violence. Do you agree with this idea? Should stricter controls be placed on the media? Why or why not?

Topic #3: If it were your job to try and convince young people between the ages of 18 and 24 to vote in local elections, what steps would you take? What do you think would be most effective?

Self-Evaluation

Use the following checklist to evaluate your work in this chapter. Mark how well that you think you have achieved this chapter's goals. Your teacher might also mark the checklist to evaluate your work. For areas marked as Needs Improvement, you should review the appropriate sections of the chapter to be sure that you get the additional practice that you need.

Goal	Excellent	Good	Needs Improvement
1. Listening to main ideas and details	_____	_____	_____
2. Consonant clusters	_____	_____	_____
3. Giving directions	_____	_____	_____
4. Making inferences	_____	_____	_____
5. Linking	_____	_____	_____
6. Persuasion	_____	_____	_____

Comments

CHAPTER 7
Creating a Career

Chapter Highlights

▶ Listening for emotions and attitudes

▶ Listening for main ideas and details

▶ Using intonation to convey attitude

▶ Describing accomplishments

▶ Guessing meaning from context

▶ Vowel length

▶ Interviewing skills

Discussion Questions

Free write, tape record, or discuss your answers to these questions with others in your class.

1. Tell your group about an experience that you or someone you know has had searching for a job.

2. Have you ever been interviewed for a job? If yes, tell the group how you felt during this experience.

Introductory Activity: Help Wanted Ads

Look at the following help wanted ads, or check similar ads in a local newspaper. Choose three ads, and complete the following chart by listing the qualifications, skills, and experience required for each position. Then discuss the questions that follow with others in your class.

Childcare/Tutor for 10 yr old boy, 5 yr old girl. Positive, energetic, driver's license, 4-8 pm M-F 555-7691

Administrative Asst.
Do you have a great attitude? Can you use word processing, spreadsheet, and desktop publishing software? Are you bilingual? If you answered yes to these questions we have a GREAT opportunity for you! Fax resume (818) 555-4567

Office Mgr
Seeking energetic, motivated professional with 3-5 yrs exp. to work in Midtown area. BA/BS degree preferred. Good compensation and benefits. Send resume to Box 2453 Midtown, CA 99119

COMPUTER
Website design
Computer sales & tech.
FT/PT. E-mail resume to job4u@get.net.

Computer application software specialist needed. Will train self-starter with basic computer literacy. Fax: (414) 555-0201

Customer Service
Established company needs well-organized, reliable person with strong communication skills. Computer literate a must. Call 555-0912

MARKETING
Int'l company seeks adventurous person to help w/ expansion. Like people? Travel? Call 999-3344

Office asst/receptionist P/T, good phone skills, computer exp. Detail oriented. 800-090-4532

Hotel Opportunities
Will train, Perm/Temp 333-222-123

Position	Qualifications	Skills	Experience

Which of the advertised jobs do you believe would be good for the following people. Explain your choices.

- High school graduate
- Student who wants to earn money for college
- College graduate
- Person with several years' work experience who wants to change careers

LISTENING ONE ▶ Toot Your Own Horn

Scott, a college junior, is thinking about summer internships and employment after graduation. His school's career center put him in touch with Ken, an alumni of Scott's college who now works for Pi Computers. Ken and Scott have exchanged a few e-mail messages, and Ken has suggested that he and Scott have lunch to talk about internships that Pi Computers offers.

Before You Listen: Describing Emotions and Attitudes

The following phrases and adjectives describe emotions or attitudes. Divide them into two lists, one for those that describe pleasant feelings and one for those that describe unpleasant feelings. Then, add any other words or phrases that you can think of that fit into each list.

I feel funny	calm
just enjoy it	at ease
stressed out	awkward
be yourself	worried
just be natural	anxious
nervous	

Pleasant Feelings	Unpleasant Feelings

You will hear some of these words and phrases in the tape that you are about to listen to.

Global Listening: Emotions and Attitudes

Listen to the conversation between Scott and Jan, and then answer the following questions.

1. At the beginning of the conversation, what is Scott's attitude toward his meeting with Ken? Why?

2. What emotions does Scott seem to be feeling during this conversation?

3. What is Jan's attitude toward Scott's meeting with Ken? Why?

4. What is Scott's attitude toward his work experience? Why?

5. At the end of the conversation, what is Scott's attitude toward his meeting? Why?

Closer Listening: Details

Now, listen to the conversation again carefully. Pay attention to the details of the conversation, and then answer the following questions.

1. What is Ken's job title?

2. What kind of job will Scott talk to Ken about?

3. How many languages does Scott speak? Does he speak them well?

4. What job experience does Scott have?

5. What computer experience does Scott have?

After You Listen: Discussion Questions

Discuss the following questions with others in your class.

1. What do you think will happen to Scott during his lunch meeting with Ken? After the meeting?

2. How would you behave at a meeting like this? How would you dress? What questions would you ask? What would you say about yourself?

With a partner, role-play the conversation that you imagine might have happened between Scott and Ken at lunch. Perform your role-play for others in your class.

Pronunciation

Using Intonation to Convey Attitude

In English, we can often predict a person's emotion or attitude by listening to the intonation of what is said. For example, consider this sentence spoken with three different intonation patterns:

I'm sure that I'll get the job.

Lightly falling intonation tells us that the speaker's comment is neutral, showing little emotion. This is the basic statement intonation pattern described in Chapter 3.

I'm sure I'll get the job.

A sharp change in intonation from high to low indicates that the speaker's comment is enthusiastic.

I'm sure I'll get the job.

A flat, low, less intense intonation with little change in pitch indicates that the speaker's comment is not genuine and instead rather sarcastic.

I'm sure I'll get the job.

Practice Hearing and Pronouncing Intonation to Convey Attitude

Listen closely to the following statements from the conversation between Scott and Jan. Write N if the statement is neutral, E if it is enthusiastic, and S if it is sarcastic. Then, rewind the tape, and repeat each statement after the speaker, trying to match the neutral, enthusiastic, or sarcastic intonation.

_____ 1. Well, I don't really know him.

_____ 2. Just go and talk to him—be yourself!

_____ 3. If I'm myself, he won't be too impressed!

_____ 4. You've worked every summer since high school.

_____ 5. Yeah, at fast food restaurants.

_____ 6. Thanks for the pep talk, Jan.

Now, try saying each sentence with a different intonation. Take a statement that is neutral on the tape and make it sarcastic. How does this change the meaning of the statement?

Practice Using Intonation to Convey Attitude

With a partner, practice reading one or both of the following dialogs. Read each one first with neutral intonation, then with enthusiastic intonation, and finally with sarcastic intonation. You might also want to read the dialog with one of you speaking enthusiastically and the other speaking sarcastically. Finally, perform the dialog for another group, using intonation to convey any of these three attitudes, or all three!

Dialog 1   A: I hear your roommate is looking for a job.
            B: Yeah. He's got a stack of resumes on the kitchen table.
            A: Has he had any luck finding anything?
            B: Not yet, but he thinks he will soon.

Dialog 2   A: So, did you decide about your major yet?
            B: No, not yet. I'm having trouble making up my mind.
            A: Maybe you should ask someone to help you.
            B: I have a meeting with my advisor on Friday.

Communicative Pronunciation Practice

With a partner, choose one of the following ending statements. For each of the situations following the statement that you choose, plan short role-plays of four to six lines each. For each situation, end the role-play with the given ending statement. You will need to pronounce the ending statement with different intonation to express different attitudes.

Ending statement A: "Sure. I can do that."

Situation #1 (neutral): Your classmate asks you to help plan a class party, and you agree.

Situation #2 (enthusiastic): You've been invited to help your classmates with a school project, and you're very excited to do so.

Situation #3 (sarcastic): A classmate asks you to do something that you are sure that you cannot do. In fact, you think it is impossible.

Ending statement B: "That sounds like a wonderful idea."

Situation #1 (neutral): A friend tells you about a present that he or she has bought to give to his or her parents. You think it is a nice present.

Situation #2 (enthusiastic): You and a friend are trying to choose a restaurant for dinner. After a lot of thinking, your friend suggests a great restaurant that you had forgotten about.

Situation #3 (sarcastic): Your friend's roommate has a problem. Your friend tells you about how the roommate plans to solve the problem, and it sounds like a bad solution to you.

Ending statement C: "Yeah, I'll be finished on time."

Situation #1 (neutral): You are writing a proposal for your boss that is due at 5:00 P.M. today. Your boss wants to know when you will finish.

Situation #2 (enthusiastic): You boss tells you that you will get a bonus if you are able to finish an important project on time and wants to know if you think that you can do it.

Situation #3 (sarcastic): A coworker tells you that the boss has moved up the deadline on the project that you are working on. You know now that you can never finish the project on time.

Interviewing Skills: Describing Accomplishments

Many people find it difficult to talk about their achievements and experiences politely, honestly, and with an appropriate amount of modesty. However, good planning and practice can help make it easier to tell others about your qualifications.

Hint #1

Talk about more than what you have done. Focus on the skills that you have developed and the personal characteristics that you have demonstrated. For example:

- When I worked at the clothing store, I really developed my customer service skills.
- To win the academic achievement award, I had to learn good time management and improve my communication skills.
- I've always enjoyed science, but I also like creating things, so I decided to study engineering.

Hint #2

Use strong action verbs that emphasize what you have done. Here are some examples of action verbs. You can find others in many books on writing resumes and cover letters.

demonstrated	completed	created	developed
organized	managed	improved	assisted

Hint #3

Review the past tense. Accomplishments are things that you *have done*, and therefore, when you talk about them, you usually must use past tense verbs. Present perfect is also very useful for talking about your recent experiences or experiences that you had at several jobs. Following is a brief review of some verb forms commonly used when talking about experience and accomplishments. If you need additional practice, consult a grammar book.

Simple Past

Simple past verb tense is used when narrating stories about the past and talking about completed actions. For example:

I graduated from college last May. I studied communications.

Past Progressive

Past progressive verb tense is used when two things happened at the same time. Usually, one verb is in the simple past and the other is in past progressive. The words *while, when,* and *during* are often used with this tense. For example:

> When I was working for the software company, I learned about many new developments in the computer industry.

> While I was a student, I was working as a research assistant for my professor.

Present Perfect

Present perfect verb tense is used when talking about something that happened not long ago or when you want to emphasize that something took place over a period of time. It is very useful when talking about your experience, whether you got that experience through your education, at one job, or with several employers. The words *already, just, recently, for,* and *since* are often used with this tense. For example:

> Ever since I was a child, I have been interested in science.

> I have recently completed a job training course.

> I have had several opportunities to coordinate office projects.

Writing a Personal Profile

Before you apply for a job, volunteer experience, or internship, you should write a personal profile. A personal profile is a document that describes your work goals, experiences, and interests. Writing a personal profile will help you to think about the special talents and skills that you have to offer an employer, as well as help you to determine what kind of job is right for you. Start by making a list of some basics.

Your skills:

_____

_____

_____

Your talents and interests:

_____

_____

_____

Your accomplishments and experience:

_____

_____

_____

Using your profile information, record a two- to three-minute description
of your accomplishments and achievements on audio tape or video tape.
Imagine that you are speaking with the director of an organization or a
company that you would like to work for. Use the suggestions for describing accomplishments to help you promote yourself!

LISTENING TWO ▶ Getting the Perfect Job

Before You Listen: Reading about Job Corps

Read the following description of Job Corps, and then answer the question
that follows.

Job Corps

Job Corps is a partnership between the U.S. government and private
companies. The agency has two purposes: first, to train young people
who otherwise may not get jobs and, second, to be sure that there are
good workers for companies to hire. Job Corps helps young people
aged 16 to 24 who are economically disadvantaged and who need
training or education in order to get a job. Seventy-three percent of
Job Corps graduates get jobs or further education. Alvin Boardley is
Director of Philadelphia Jobs Corps and has a lot of advice for young
people who are looking for work.

What advice do you expect Mr. Boardley to give to jobseekers? Write your
predictions on the following lines, and then share your ideas with others in
your class.

1. _____

2. _____

3. _____

Global Listening: Main Ideas

Read the following list of suggestions. Then, listen to the suggestions that Alvin Boardley makes and check each one in the following list that you hear. Compare the suggestions that you heard to the predictions that you made previously.

   _____   1. Learn as much as you can.
   _____   2. Learn to operate a computer.
   _____   3. Act like you know all of the answers.
   _____   4. Know what employers expect.
   _____   5. Organize your resume and work history.
   _____   6. Research the company before the interview.
   _____   7. Appear to be humble.
   _____   8. Appear to be self-confident.
   _____   9. Video tape a practice interview, and critique yourself.
   _____ 10. Practice interviewing with friends.

Closer Listening: Guessing Meaning from Context

In this interview, Mr. Boardley uses some idiomatic language, but usually you can guess the meanings of these phrases from context. Listen to the interview again, paying special attention to the following quotes. In your own words, paraphrase the quote by using simpler words and language. The first one is done for you.

1. You certainly can't go wrong by being overqualified with regard to your academic level.

   It is a good idea to get as much education as possible.

2. I think one of the big common mistakes is that they think they know it all, uh, or they have all the answers to the questions, uh and you know they're, or they're too cocky ... .

   _____

3. They don't do their homework, ...

   _____

4. At least that will get you in the door ... .

   _____

5. Friends that are open and honest and willing to tell you like it is, not friends who are gonna tell you what you wanna hear.

   _____

Cultural Notes: Promoting Yourself

In North American culture, children are taught from a very young age to "toot their own horns," to be able to speak with ease about themselves and their accomplishments whether in social situations, such as making small talk at a party, or more formal settings such as a job interview.

In a job interview, it is important that you seem self-confident without bragging or being arrogant. This is difficult because, as mentioned in the listening, there is a "fine line" between being self-confident and seeming "cocky" (overly confident or boastful).

For each response to the following question, say whether you think that the statement is too humble, too cocky, or self-confident. After you have finished, compare your answers with a classmate's. Check with your teacher if you have any questions.

Question: Do you have any experience using computers?

Answer #1: Yes, I feel very confident using computers and understand how to use many different kinds of office software for word processing, database management, and, of course, working with e-mail.

_____

Answer #2: Well, not much really, I used computers during school, and I have a computer at home, but that's about it.

_____

Answer #3: I love computers! I am up-to-date on all of the latest software, and I am constantly upgrading my computer at home—it's my passion!

_____

Pronunciation

Vowel Length

To speak English clearly, it is important that you pronounce vowel sounds correctly. In some words, however, English speakers listen not just for the sound of the vowel, but also for the length of the vowel. Fortunately, the rules for vowel length are fairly easy to learn and practice.

A vowel sound followed by a voiced consonant will be lengthened. The same vowel followed by a voiceless consonant will be shorter. It actually takes more time to say the lengthened vowel sound that is followed by the voiced consonant. This is most evident in one-syllable words such as those in the following table.

Lengthened Vowel	Shortened Vowel
cab	cap
made	mate
buzz	bus
badge	batch

In these words, the length of the vowel sound is the most important clue that listeners have to determine which word has been spoken.

Note: Vowel length refers to the time that it takes to say the *same vowel sound* when followed by different consonant sounds. It is different from *vowel pairs* such as /iy/ and /ɪ/, which some people call *long i* and *short i*.

Practice Predicting Vowel Length

Review the following phrases from the interview with Alvin Boardley. In each phrase, one word is in italics. Look at the vowel in this word. Based on the consonant sound that follows this vowel, predict whether this word has long or short vowel length. Circle your prediction. Remember to focus on the sounds in the word and not the spelling.

1. when you *look* at the changing global marketplace   Short   Long

2. try to learn as *much* as you can   Short   Long

3. one of the *big* common mistakes   Short   Long

4. going in for a *job* interview   Short   Long

5. the *type* of attire they wear   Short   Long

6. so that it looks real *good*   Short   Long

7. this is the *bright* person that I'm looking for   Short   Long

8. I think it's uh a very *thin* line   Short   Long

Practice Listening to Vowel Length

Now, listen to the phrases again, paying particular attention to the italicized word to hear whether it has short or long vowel length. Circle your answer. Then, compare your answers with your previous predictions.

1. when you *look* at the changing global marketplace   Short   Long

2. try to learn as *much* as you can   Short   Long

3. one of the *big* common mistakes   Short   Long

4. going in for a *job* interview   Short   Long

5. the *type* of attire they wear   Short   Long

6. so that it looks real *good*   Short   Long

7. this is the *bright* person that I'm looking for   Short   Long

8. I think it's uh a very *thin* line   Short   Long

Practice Pronouncing Voiced and Voiceless Consonants

This activity will help you to learn if you have trouble pronouncing vowel length correctly. Work with a small group of classmates, and secretly choose one sentence from each pair and read it to your group. Your classmates will read the end of the sentence that they think they have heard. If the group cannot easily decide which is the correct ending to your sentence from column B, ask your teacher. You might have mispronounced the sound, or your classmates might have misheard the sound.

Column A   Column B

/p/ and /b/

In her lap ...   she held a fat cat.
In her lab ...   she does experiments.

/s/ and /z/

He wants peas ...   for dinner.
He wants peace ...   on Earth.

/k/ and /g/

Put that in the back ...   of the car.
Put that in the bag, ...   and then close the bag.

/f/ and /v/

| He said, "Life ... | is full of surprises." |
| He said, "Live ... | TV is exciting." |

/tʃ/ and /dʒ/

| They gave a badge ... | to the new police officer. |
| They gave a batch ... | of cookies to the kindergarten children. |

Communicative Pronunciation Practice

Follow these steps to practice pronouncing vowel length.

1. What do you hope to have achieved one year, five years, and ten years from now? Make a list of these goals. On your list, circle ten one-syllable words. For each word, determine whether the vowel length is long or short.

2. It is ten years in the future, and now you have attained all of the goals on your list. You have been invited back to your school to give a speech to current students. Plan what you will say to introduce yourself to these students. Be sure that your introduction includes all of the accomplishments that you hope to have achieved ten years from now.

3. Record your introduction. Be careful to pronounce vowel length correctly, especially in the ten words that you chose in step one. Then listen carefully to your recording to see if you made any mistakes with these sounds.

TALK It Through!

Interviewing Skills: Tips for Answering Interview Questions

In Chapter 3, you learned about how to ask questions to interview someone. Sometimes, however, you might be answering the questions in the interview. This requires a different kind of preparation. When answering interview questions, always remember the following helpful hints.

1. Listen carefully to the question so that you understand exactly what the interviewer is asking.

2. Give yourself a moment to think before giving your answer. This will give you a little time to organize your thoughts and ideas. Begin by restating or rephrasing the question to introduce your answer. You

might also want to preface your restatement by commenting on the question. For example:

Question: What do you think is the most important quality or skill to have today if you are looking for a job in education?

Answer: Hmm, that's an interesting question. I think the most important quality or skill for educators today is … .

3. In your answer, give as many specific facts and examples as possible. For example:

   Question: Do you have experience working with children?

   Answer: Yes, I've been working with children ages three to six for the past three years at Magic Land Day Care Center. I was responsible for organizing their reading hour, special activities … . I also coordinated their day trips to the library and the local park. I really loved this experience.

4. Be positive! Avoid negative statements such as "I can't," "that's a difficult question," and "I don't know." Try to use the intonation strategies that you learned earlier in the chapter to express your enthusiasm in your answers.

Identifying What Interviewers Want

You cannot know ahead of time what questions you will be asked in a job interview, but you can make some very good assumptions. To predict interview questions, follow these steps.

1. Review the section on conducting interviews in Chapter 3 on pages 46–48.

2. Find an advertisement for a job in a newspaper or on the Internet.

3. Think about what this employer would want to know about a potential employee.

4. Use the following list to write questions that employers might ask.

What do employers want to know about an employee?

_____

_____

_____

_____

What questions should an interviewee anticipate?

_____

_____

_____

_____

Practicing Interviewing Skills

Every interview is different, but some questions are very common. Following are some likely questions that you would be asked. Choose at least three, and brainstorm appropriate answers with a partner or small group of your classmates.

What motivates you in a job and in your personal life?

Describe the perfect job.

What are your five biggest accomplishments?

If you could change something about your life, what would that be?

What goals have you set for yourself? Why did you choose these?

Describe your ideal picture of success.

Describe your personality.

Describe your work habits.

What are your strengths?

What are your weaknesses?

Practice your interviewing skills with a classmate. Follow these steps.

1. Choose a job description from a newspaper or the Internet. You might want to use the one that you used in the previous activity.

2. Select some questions from the previous list or from your own list of questions.

3. Take turns with a partner being the interviewer and the interviewee.

4. When you are the interviewer, ask the question and then give the interviewee 45 seconds to answer it.

5. When you are the interviewee, follow the tips described in the box on pages 128–129. Also, be persuasive. Refer to pages 110–111 in Chapter 6 if you need to review tips on how to persuade.

6. Remember, Alvin Boardley said that only honest critiques from friends are helpful. Give to your partner feedback that you think will help your partner. You might want to video tape your interviews so that you can evaluate your interviewing skills.

Using the Internet

There are many sites on the Internet that give good advice about resume writing and job interviews. Use any search engine to find one of these sites, and then give a brief presentation to a group of your classmates in which you summarize the information that you found on the site.

Occupations and the Skills That They Require

When thinking about a future career, it is important that you consider the types of jobs that are available and the skills that you need to do these jobs effectively. Over the next decade, people in the following occupations will be in high demand. Complete the following chart by writing the skills that you think that you would need in order to effectively do each job.

Occupation	Skills
Elementary school teacher	A degree in elementary education, teaching certification, good with children, creative
Emergency medical technician	
Computer programmer	
Paralegal	
Electrical engineer	
Marketing manager	
Graphic designer	
Social worker	

After completing the previous chart, discuss the following questions with other classmates.

1. If you had to work in one of these occupations, which one would it be? Why?

2. What is your "dream career"? What are the special skills that you need for this career? What are the benefits of this career?

3. If you are currently working, tell what you like about your career. What career would you choose if you could change careers?

Self-Evaluation

Use the following checklist to evaluate your work in this chapter. Mark how well you think that you have achieved this chapter's goals. Your teacher might also mark the checklist to evaluate your work. For areas marked as Needs Improvement, you should review the appropriate sections of the chapter to be sure that you get the additional practice that you need.

Goal	Excellent	Good	Needs Improvement
1. Listening for emotions and attitudes	_____	_____	_____
2. Listening for main ideas and details	_____	_____	_____
3. Using intonation to convey attitude	_____	_____	_____
5. Describing accomplishments	_____	_____	_____
6. Guessing meaning from context	_____	_____	_____
7. Vowel length	_____	_____	_____
8. Interviewing skills	_____	_____	_____

Comments

CHAPTER 8
Science or Fiction?

Chapter Highlights

▶ Listening for main ideas

▶ Identifying justifications

▶ Vowel sounds with glides

▶ Expressing disagreement

▶ Drawing conclusions

▶ Intonation for lists and choices

▶ Conducting a survey

Discussion Questions

Free write, tape record, or discuss your answers to these questions with others in your class.

1. What science classes have you taken? Do you enjoy studying science? Why or why not?

2. Do you believe that science is the only way to find the truth about the world around us? Why or why not?

3. What are some things that people believe that cannot yet be proved by science? Do you believe in any of these things? Why or why not?

Introductory Activity: Categories of Theories

The following famous quotation from a play by William Shakespeare means that science and philosophy cannot understand or explain many things. Do you agree or disagree with this quotation?

"There are more things in heaven and earth, Horatio, than are dreamt of in your philosophy." —*Hamlet*, Act 1, Scene 5

Ideas about how the world works fit into three categories, as depicted in the following diagram.

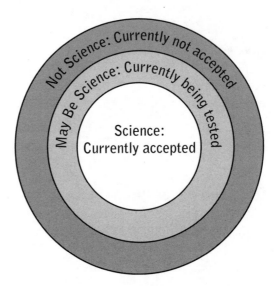

Look at the following list of ideas. Into which of the three categories do you think that each falls? In the chart that follows, write the letter of the idea in the appropriate space. Compare your answers with others in your class, and give reasons to support your choices.

a. The big bang theory: The idea that the universe started with one big explosion

b. Palm reading: Predicting someone's future by reading the lines in their hands

c. Acupuncture: The process of healing diseases by inserting needles at specific points on the body

d. UFO abduction theory: Aliens take humans to perform experiments on them

e. Cloning: Using a cell from one animal to make another animal just like the first

f. Hypnosis: An altered mental state in which behavior can be changed or psychological problems explored

g. Global warming: The temperature of Earth is rising because of pollution

h. Extrasensory perception (ESP): The ability to know things that you couldn't have discovered with your five senses of sight, hearing, touch, taste, and smell

i. Astrology: Learning one's personality or future from the position of the stars when you were born

j. Psychoanalysis: Working with an analyst to solve psychological problems by finding the childhood event or memory that caused the problem

Categories	Ideas That You Think Belong in This Category
Science: Currently accepted	
May be science: Currently being tested	
Not science: Currently not accepted	

Sara is visiting her friend Jason during a school vacation. They have planned to go out for the afternoon, and Sara is at the door, ready to leave. Jason is sitting at his computer checking his horoscope.

Before You Listen: Pseudoscience

Before you listen to Sara and Jason's conversation, read the information on pseudoscience in the following box.

What Is Pseudoscience?

The prefix "pseudo" means "fake or unreal." So pseudoscience means fake science. The *Skeptic's Dictionary*[1] defines pseudoscience in this way: "A pseudoscience is a set of ideas based on theories put forth as scientific when they are *not* scientific."

For example, many people believe that ESP, astrology, UFO abductions, and some forms of alternative medicine are pseudoscience. Others believe that these are very real phenomena that simply have not yet been proved scientifically. Some people believe in these phenomena because of

- tradition (my family has always believed in it),
- faith (I don't need proof to know that it is true), or
- evidence or experience that they feel supports its existence.

[1] *http://www.dcn.davis.ca.us/~btcarrol/skeptic/pseudosc.html* or *SkepDic.com*.

Global Listening: Main Ideas

Listen to the dialogue between Sara and Jason. Then, complete each of the following sentences based on the information in the conversation.

1. Sara thinks that astrology is _____.

2. Jason thinks that astrology is _____.

3. Jason says that many people _____.

4. Jason's evidence that horoscopes work is that _____

   _____.

~~~~
Aquarius

♓
Pisces

♈
Aries

♉
Taurus

♊
Gemini

♋
Cancer

♌
Leo

♍
Virgo

♎
Libra

♏
Scorpio

♐
Sagittarius

♑
Capricorn

Closer Listening: Identifying Justifications

 Listen to the tape again. This time, listen carefully to how Sara and Jason justify their opinions about astrology. Note these justifications in the following chart.

Sara's Justifications	Jason's Justifications

After You Listen: Discussion Questions

Discuss the following questions with others in your class.

1. What reason does Jason give for believing in astrology: tradition, faith, or evidence? How do you know?

2. What is your opinion about astrology? Do you agree with Jason or Sara? Why?

3. How do people from your culture try to predict the future? Describe how these methods work. Has this method ever worked for you?

Vowel Sounds with Glides

Several vowels in English have little *glides* at the end of the sound. Glides are made by adding a /y/ or a /w/ at the end of a vowel sound. Glides not only make the end of the vowel sound different, but also make the vowel longer. Learning to make these glides on these vowel sounds can help you to make your speech more comprehensible, since some of the sounds are easily confused with similar vowel sounds that have no glides.

Vowel sounds can have a /y/ glide or a /w/ glide at the end of the sound. Those with glides include the following:

/iy/ as in <u>see</u>   /ow/ as in <u>so</u>

/ey/ as in <u>say</u>   /uw/ as in <u>sue</u>

In *Talk It Through!*, we write the symbols for these sounds with the /y/ and the /w/ symbol to help remind you to pronounce these sounds with a glide.

To help you to understand the difference between vowels with /y/ and /w/ glides and those without, compare the following word pairs. In each, the sound with the glide is given first.

/iy/   /ɪ/   /ey/   /ɛ/   /ow/   /ɑ/   /uw/   /ʊ/

leave   live   main   men   note   knot   food   foot

Determining Whether These Sounds Are Difficult for You to Pronounce

This exercise will help you to learn whether you pronounce vowel sounds with glides clearly and accurately. Secretly choose one sentence from each pair and read it to your group. Your classmates will read the end of the sentence that they think they have heard. If the group cannot easily decide which is the correct ending to your sentence from column B, ask your teacher. You might have mispronounced the sound, or your classmates might have misheard the sound.

Column A	Column B
/iy/ and /ɪ/	
When did you live ...	with your parents?
When did you leave ...	the party last night?
/ey/ and /ɛ/	
I thought the men ...	would be here by now.
I thought the main ...	problem was money.

/ow/ and /ɑ/

She made a note ...	of the correct answer.
She made a knot ...	in her shoelace and couldn't untie it.

/uw/ and /ʊ/

They should ...	practice every day.
They shooed ...	away the bugs that were bothering them.

Practice Listening to and Pronouncing Vowel Sounds That Have Glides

Look at the following sentences from the dialog between Jason and Sara, and predict which words contain vowel sounds that have glides. Then, listen again to the tape and circle each word that has a vowel sound with a glide.

1. I mean, none of it has ever been proven. It's totally unscientific.

2. Well, I'm not the only one who believes. Lots of people read their horoscopes everyday.

3. Lots of people believe that aliens have landed in New Mexico.

4. I would love to be able to know what will happen to me in the future.

5. You're crazy! Let's go. You're gonna miss that bus.

Now, rewind the tape and repeat each sentence after the speaker, being careful to pronounce the glide after each vowel sound.

Communicative Pronunciation Practice

Learn ten new words about a subject of interest to you, and teach these words to the class. Follow these steps to do this.

1. Choose a science or a subject that some people consider to be pseudoscience. You might select a science such as biology, chemistry, or physics, or you could look into astrology, UFOs, ESP, or some other field that interests you.

2. Learn the new words, either by interviewing someone with experience in the area or by using the Internet, a magazine, or book on the topic. Find out the definition of each word, and write a sample sentence using the word. Practice the correct pronunciation of each, paying particular attention to the vowel sounds.

3. Teach your words to your classmates, either in small groups or by using audio tape. As you are teaching the new words, be sure to pronounce the vowel sounds correctly.

Conversational Skills: Expressing Disagreement

When talking about controversial topics, people often find that their opinions about the topic differ—they disagree. Disagreeing does not mean that they are angry or fighting; usually people are able to explain their disagreements without becoming upset. (Of course, sometimes people do get angry when others disagree with them. Expressing and responding to anger is discussed in Chapter 5.)

We are more likely to express our disagreement more freely with our friends, family, and peers than we are with strangers or superiors. When expressing disagreement with strangers or superiors, we generally use indirect phrases such as the following.

I haven't seen any evidence to prove that yet.

I'm not sure that I would agree with you on that point.

That hasn't been true in my experience.

In less formal situations, such as those involving family, friends, and peers, we might use such phrases as the following.

Well, that's not the way that I see it.

Oh, I don't think that's true.

Do you really believe that?

I'm surprised to hear you say that.

I disagree because … .

I don't know about that. It doesn't sound right to me.

Sometimes people disagree with each other simply by stating their opinions or offering evidence that disagrees with the other person's opinion. For example, read the responses to the following opinions.

Opinion: All fortune-tellers are liars.

Disagreement: I don't know. I read about Madame Simeon, who could tell the future, and no scientist has ever been able to prove that she was cheating or lying.

Opinion: Time travel is definitely possible in the future.

Disagreement: Well, I think if time travel was possible in the future, someone would have already come back from the future and told us about it.

Important note: Remember that sometimes it is not *what* you say but *how* you say it. Some people express disagreement through sarcasm. That is, the words that they use seem to indicate agreement, but the way that they stress words in the sentence and the intonation that they use convey the exact opposite meaning. For example,

Oh! That was *really* smart!

means it was not smart at all.

Any of the previous phrases could sound rude if sarcastic word stress and intonation are used. To review sarcastic intonation, see Chapter 7, page 118.

Listening to the Language

Rewind the tape and listen again to the conversation between Jason and Sara. This time, after you listen to a few lines, stop the tape and continue the conversation with a partner. You may finish the conversation in the same way or make up your own ending. Try to use as many phrases for disagreeing as you can.

Role-Play Situations for Disagreeing

Choose one of the following statements, and with a partner, make a list of comments that agree with the statement and a list that disagree with the statement. Then, create a role-play in which one of you agrees with the statement and the other disagrees. Remember that it is very good speaking practice to defend an opinion that you don't really agree with.

1. Women's sports will never be as interesting as men's sports.

2. Even if there is life on other planets, we will never know about it.

3. You can tell a lot about a person just by looking at that person's handwriting.

4. Fortune tellers and palm readers are just for entertainment and don't give any useful information.

5. Advertising doesn't affect me. I don't buy things just because I see them in an ad.

6. Computers are already smarter than most humans.

Mark Abrams is a scientist working at Harvard University. He is also the editor of the *Annals of Improbable Research,* a journal that publishes unusual scientific research. The journal's Web site is at *http://www.improb.com/.* Dr. Abrams believes that even studies on topics that seem silly can still be scientific. And he has seen some very peculiar studies.

Before You Listen: The Scientific Method

The scientific method is a process that people use when they are trying to solve a problem logically or when they are trying to discover the answer to a question about the world around us. The following diagram depicts the scientific method.

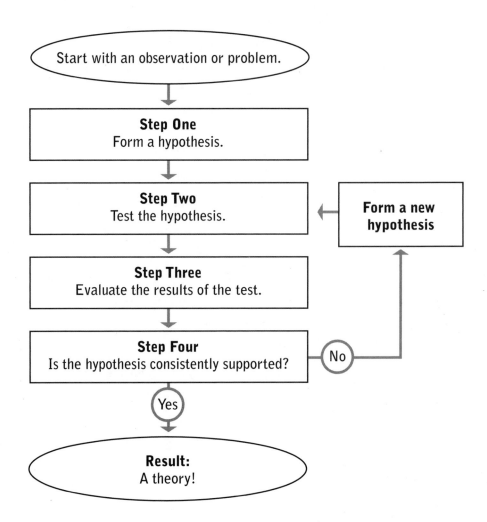

Use the scientific method to put the problem-solving steps for each of the following observations in the correct order.

Observation: When you turn on the light switch, the lights don't come on.

_____ Hypothesis

_____ Test

_____ Evaluation

_____ Evidence for or against the hypothesis

a.   No other appliances work, so the electricity in the house must not be working.

b.   Try turning on other appliances in the house.

c.   The electricity in the house is not working.

d.   See if the appliances work when turned on.

Observation: You don't know how long it takes to cook a potato in the microwave on full power.

_____ Hypothesis

_____ Test

_____ Evaluation

_____ Evidence for or against the hypothesis

a.   It will take four minutes at full power.

b.   Use a fork to find out if the potato is soft in the center.

c.   Put the potato in the oven, and turn it on full power for four minutes.

d.   The potato is not soft in the center, so four minutes at full power is not enough to cook a potato in the microwave.

Now, with a group of your classmates, determine the steps for forming a hypothesis and testing these everyday observations by using the scientific method.

Observation: Your houseplant does not look healthy.

Observation: Some food you made does not have enough flavor.

Observation: Your test grades are not as high as you would like.

Your own observation: _____

_____

Global Listening: Main Ideas

Listen to the conversation with Mark Abrams, and try to determine the answer to this question: "What is science?" You might want to take notes while you listen. Then, summarize your answer in one or two sentences and write them in the following lines.

_____

_____

Closer Listening: Drawing Conclusions

Listen to the tape a second time, this time looking at the diagram of the scientific method on page 142. You will need to use the information both from the diagram and the listening to answer the following questions. Using information from more than one source to determine the answer to questions is called drawing conclusions.

1. At the start of the conversation, Dr. Abrams mentions three studies. Are these three studies science? Why do you think so? Why not?

2. Which step of the scientific method does Dr. Abrams emphasize in this conversation? How do you know?

3. Was the hypothesis of the Japanese scientists who studied pigeons and paintings supported? How do you know?

After You Listen: Is It Science or Science Fiction?

For each of the following topics, decide whether you think that the topic is scientifically possible (or will be someday) or is science fiction. Discuss your answers with others in your class.

Topic	Science?	Science Fiction?
Human cloning		
Time travel		
Life on other planets		
Computers that are more intelligent than humans		
Repairing the hole in the ozone		
Humans living on the moon or Mars		

Pronunciation

Intonation for Lists and Choices

In Chapter 3 you learned that intonation is the rising or falling pitch of your voice when you speak. That is, as you speak, the sound of your voice constantly becomes higher and lower. Every thought group in English has an intonation pattern. Intonation is very important when you are participating in a discussion because it often signals the kind of information that you are giving.

For example, when a speaker lists two or more points or ideas, intonation lets the listener know when the list begins and when it ends. When you are listing, the pitch goes up for each point except the last one. On the last point, the pitch goes down, thereby signaling the end of the list. For example:

When you come for your appointment, please bring your driver's license,

your birth certificate, and two hundred and fifty dollars.

Listing intonation is also used with longer phrases and clauses. For example:

When I moved into my house, I did a lot of work.

I painted all of the walls bright green,

I planted flowers and trees in the garden,

and I got the place checked out for termites.

Intonation can also be used in a sentence to signal choice. When a choice between two alternatives is offered, the pitch goes up on the first alternative and goes down on the second. For example:

Should I take accounting or finance?

We can take the train or the bus.

Practice Listening to Intonation for Lists and Choices

Listen to the following sentences from Listening One, and mark with upward and downward arrows the intonation that you hear. Check what you have heard with a partner. Then practice saying the sentences, imitating the speakers' intonation for listings and choices.

1. The way that it goes from being nice, crisp, crunchy cereal to something that is just full of milk.

2. They showed these paintings to some pigeons, and they're trying to figure out whether they could teach the pigeons to tell the difference between a painting that was painted by Monet and a painting that was painted by Picasso.

3. Are you gonna believe a story that somebody else told you: your neighbor, your father, the kid next door says UFOs come by at night. Is that true? Is it true just because he told you? Or can you find some way to figure out for yourself and test it, and see whether it's true?

4. So, if you, if you try to test it, and bounce it against the facts that you already know, then you're doing science.

Practice Pronouncing Intonation for Lists and Choices

The following geography quiz questions all suggest three possible answers, but only one is right. First, write a similar geography question and offer three choices for the answer. One of the choices should be correct. Then, practice reading the questions with a partner. As you ask and answer the questions, try to use the correct listing and choice intonation.

1. Which city has the largest population: Los Angeles, Seoul, or Rio de Janeiro?

2. Is the capital city of Canada Ottawa or Montreal?

3. Is the city of Caracas in Equador, Colombia, or Venezuela?

4. Which country does not border the Red Sea: Egypt, Libya, or Saudi Arabia?

5. Which country has a colder climate: Greenland or Iceland?

6. The country of Germany is bordered by which nine countries?

7. What are the three largest countries in South America?

8. Mongolia borders which two countries?

9. What are the five largest countries in the world in terms of population?

10. Where is the city of Katmandu? In Burma, Nepal, or Pakistan?

11. _____

12. _____

Communicative Pronunciation Practice

In our everyday lives, we encounter problems for which we have to find solutions. For example, we need to figure out how to program our VCRs, how to use a particular type of computer software, or how to get to a new location by using public transportation. Describe a problem that you have encountered in your daily life or at home, school, or work, and give a solution to this problem. This solution should include lists of options and choices. For example:

Problem description: I often need to do banking, but I don't have much time during banking hours.

Solution: I can walk to the bank during my lunch break, bank by phone, or bank on-line by using the bank's Web site. The good thing about banking on-line is that it's fast and convenient and I can print a record of all of my transactions. The downside to on-line banking is security. I'm not sure it's safe—I don't trust sending my personal information over the Internet—and I've heard of people having problems with my bank's on-line system. Going to the bank personally is fun; I find the staff pleasant and hardworking. The problem there is often very long lines. So I guess the best option for me is banking by phone. I am charged one dollar every time that I use the service, but I can finish everything I need to do in a few minutes, and I trust the system.

As you prepare your problem description and solution, be aware of the intonation for listings and choices that you will need to use when you read them aloud. When you have finished, practice reading them aloud, paying close attention to intonation for listings and choices. When you feel comfortable with your efforts, present your work to your classmates or audio tape record it so that you or your teacher can check your intonation.

Presentation Skills: Conducting a Survey

By now, you have probably realized that not only scientists use the scientific method to answer questions and solve problems. One type of scientific study often used by social scientists, advertisers, and politicians is the *survey*. You listened to a part of a survey in Chapter 5, when people in New Jersey were asked their opinions about tabloids. A survey is used when someone wants to learn the opinions or habits of a large group of people in a short amount of time. Many scientific and statistical rules must be followed in order for a survey to be considered scientifically valid. For example, if you cannot survey all of the people in the target group, you must be sure to get a random sample large enough to represent the entire group. The questions that you ask in the survey also must be very carefully planned and worded.

A survey that you do in this class will probably not stand up to testing by other scientists, but you can use a survey to practice your speaking and listening skills, while at the same time learning something about the people around you. Here are some tips to help you.

- Narrow your topic. Do not try to answer a broad question such as, "How many Canadians believe in pseudoscience?" You would have to ask a lot of people and a lot of questions to find the answer to this question. Instead, choose a topic like: "Do many people in our community believe in UFOs?"
- Write your topic in the form of a question, or develop a hypothesis predicting the result.

  Example question: Do students in this school usually do more than three hours of homework each school night?

  Example hypothesis: Students in this school usually do more than three hours of homework each night.

- Decide which group of people you will survey, such as members of a certain profession, organization, age group, location, or even people that share a particular interest.
- Ask closed-ended questions because people will give short answers to them that are easy to count. Examples are yes/no questions and questions starting with *who, what, when,* and *where.*

Conducting a Survey

As a class, conduct a survey in your community to find out what people think is pseudoscience. Follow these steps.

1. As a class, write a hypothesis predicting what your survey will find.

2. You will ask people if they believe in astrology/horoscopes, UFOs, and/or ESP and record the results in the chart following these instructions. Add a fourth area that you want to ask about, and write it in the space in the chart.

3. Plan and practice the questions that you will ask people. Practice using the correct question intonation.

4. Each class member should ask five people to answer the questions in the survey.

5. When you ask your questions, be sure to ask each respondent to participate politely. Say something such as, "Would you help me with a project for my English class by answering a few questions?"

6. Record each respondent's answers in the chart that follows these instructions.

7. Make a master chart that shows the total answers that everyone received, and prepare an analysis of the results. Report your results to the class.

8. Determine whether your hypothesis was supported. Remember that it is not bad if your hypothesis is *not* supported. Regardless of whether it is supported, your survey gives you facts that you can use to form an opinion—or a new hypothesis.

9. List the reasons that your information might not be completely accurate. This is an important part of a scientific report. For example: We asked only 75 people, so this survey can't tell us about trends all across the United States.

Topic	Believe	Do Not Believe	Reasons for Belief or Disbelief
Astrology/horoscopes			
UFOs			
ESP			

Is Your Survey Science?

How does the survey that you conducted follow the scientific method? The steps of the method are listed next. Beside each step, write how you followed the step when conducting your survey. If you didn't follow the step, write what you should have done to follow the scientific method.

Make an observation/ask a question:

_____

Form a hypothesis:

_____

Test the hypothesis:

_____

Analyze the results:

_____

Recall the interview with Dr. Abrams. Do you think that he would consider your survey to be science? Why or why not?

Evaluating Sources

Web sites give information on a variety of subjects. However, this information can be misguided, misleading, or completely untrue! To be sure that the information that you are getting is accurate, you need to think critically about the Web site. Use the following checklist to evaluate Web sites.

- Check the source of the information (who takes responsibility for it), the date that the site was posted, and whether it has been updated recently.
- Check whether it has been cited by other authors who write about the same topic.
- Check the accuracy of the sources that the site's authors use to get information. A credible, believable site will list those sources.
- Beware of any strong or radical opinions that are not supported by facts.
- Remember the scientific method. Use it to check any doubts that you have about the information on the site.

Search the Internet to find several Web pages on a subject of interest to you. You may choose one of the subjects, science or pseudoscience, mentioned in this chapter. Choose one page that you think is credible and one that you think is not. Judge each page using the checklist in the preceding box. Then, report on your findings to a group of your classmates.

Self-Evaluation

Use the following checklist to evaluate your work in this chapter. Mark how well you think that you have achieved this chapter's goals. Your teacher might also mark the checklist to evaluate your work. For areas marked as Needs Improvement, you should review the appropriate sections of the chapter to be sure that you get the additional practice that you need.

Goal	Excellent	Good	Needs Improvement
1. Listening for main ideas and details	_____	_____	_____
2. Identifying justifications	_____	_____	_____
3. Vowel sounds with glides	_____	_____	_____
4. Expressing disagreement	_____	_____	_____
5. Drawing conclusions	_____	_____	_____
6. Intonation for lists and choices	_____	_____	_____
7. Conducting a survey	_____	_____	_____

Comments